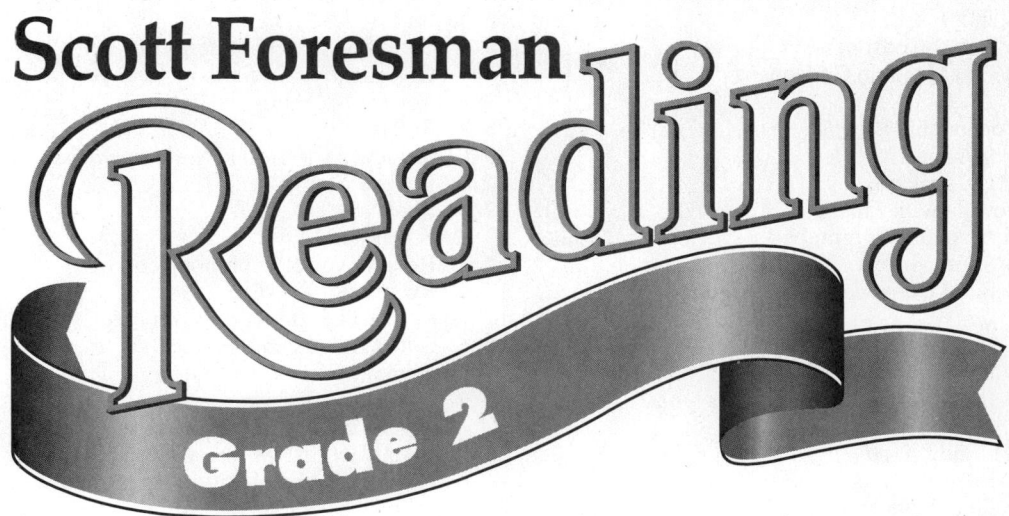

Phonics Workbook
Blackline Master
and Answer Key

Scott Foresman

Editorial Offices: Glenview, Illinois • New York, New York
Sales Offices: Reading, Massachusetts • Duluth, Georgia • Glenview, Illinois
Carrollton, Texas • Menlo Park, California

Table of Contents

Skill	Page Numbers
Short *a, i, u*	1-2
l, r, s Blends	3
Review Initial Consonants *g* /j/, *c* /s/	4
Review Final Double Consonants	5
Short *e, o*	6-7
Final Consonants Blends	8
Review Consonants *c, k, ck*	9
Review *l, r, s* Blends	10
Long Vowels with Final *e*	11-12
Initial Consonants Digraphs	13
Review Short Vowels	14
Review Final Consonant Blends	15
Long *e: ea, ee*	16-17
Final Consonant Digraphs	18
Review Long Vowels with Final *e*	19
Review Initial Consonant Digraphs	20
Long *e: e, y*	21-22
Inflected Ending *-ed*	23
Review Long *e: ea, ee*	24
Review Final Consonant Digraphs	25
Long *a: a, ai, ay*	26-27
Inflected Endings *-es, -ing,* and *-s*	28
Review Long *e: e, y*	29
Review Inflected Ending *-ed*	30
Long *i: i, igh, y, ie*	31-32
Medial Consonants	33
Review Long *a: a, ai, ay*	34
Review Inflected Endings *-es, -ing,* and *-s*	35
r-Controlled Vowels *er, ir, ur*	36-37
Plurals *-s* and *-es*	38
Review Long *i: i, igh, y,* and *ie*	39
Review Medial Consonants	40
Long *o: o, oa, ow, oe*	41-42
Compound Words	43
Review *r*-Controlled Vowels: *er, ir, ur*	44
Plurals *-s* and *-es*	45
Words with *ce, ge, se*	46-47
Possessives	48
Review Long *o: o, oa, ow, oe*	49
Compound Words	50
Vowel Diphthongs *ou, ow*	51-52
Inflected Endings	53
Words with *ce, ge, se*	54
Review Possessives	55
r-Controlled Vowel: *ar*	56-57
Inflected Endings	58
Review Vowel Diphthongs *ou, ow*	59
Inflected Endings	60
Sound of Vowel Patterns *ew, oo, ou*	61-62
Contractions	63
Review *r*-Controlled Vowel: *ar*	64
Inflected Endings	65
r-Controlled Vowels: *or, ore, oor, our*	66-67
Inflected Endings	68
Review Sound of Vowel Patterns *ew, oo, ou*	69
Contractions	70
Sound of Vowel Patterns *oo, ou*	71-72
Comparative Endings *-er, -est*	73
Review *r*-Controlled Vowels: *or, ore, oor, our*	74
Inflected Endings	75

Skill	Page Numbers
r-Controlled Vowels: *ear, eer*	76-77
Suffix *-ly*	78
Sound of Vowels Patterns *oo, ou*	79
Comparative Endings *-er, -est*	80
Vowel Diphthongs *oi, oy*	81-82
Suffix *-ful*	83
Review *r*-Controlled Vowels: *ear, eer*	84
Review Suffix *-ly*	85
Short *e: ea*	86-87
Suffix *-er*	88
Review Vowel Diphthongs *oi, oy*	89
Review Suffix *-ful*	90
/ȯ/ Vowel Patterns *a, al, au*	91-92
Silent Letters: *kn, mb*	93
Review Short *e: ea*	94
Review Suffix *-er*	95
/ȯ/ Vowel Patterns *aw, ough*	96-97
Silent Letters: *gn, wh, wr*	98
Review /ȯ/ Vowel Patterns *a, al, au*	99
Review Silent Letters: *kn, mb*	100
Short *u: ou*	101-102
Multisyllabic Words	103
Review /ȯ/ Vowel Patterns *aw, ough*	104
Review Silent Letters: *gn, wh, wr*	105
Schwa Sound in *across* and *people*	106-107
Plural *-s* and *-es*	108
Review Short *u: ou*	109
Review Multisyllabic Words	110
Vowel Digraph *ue*	111-112
Schwa Sound in *weather*	113
Review Schwa Sound in *across* and *people*	114
Review Plural *-s* and *-es*	115
Long *a: ei, eigh*	116-117
Words with Endings and Suffixes	118
Review Vowel Digraph *ue*	119
Review Schwa Sound in *weather*	120
Pattern *ex*	121-122
Prefixes *un-, dis-, re-*	123
Review Long *a: ei, eigh*	124
Words with Endings and Suffixes	125
Long *e: ie, ey*	126-127
Consonants *gh, ph, lf* /f/	128
Review Pattern *ex*	129
Prefixes *un-, dis-, re-*	130
Long *e: ei*	131-132
Plural *-es*	133
Review Long *e: ie, ey*	134
Review Consonants *gh, ph, lf* /f/	135
r-Controlled vowels: *air, are*	136-137
Consonants: *dge* /j/	138
Review Long *e: ei*	139
Review Plurals *-es*	140
Long Vowels at the Ends of Syllables	141-142
Consonants *ch* /k/, *sch* /sk/	143
r-Controlled Vowels: *air, are*	144
Review Consonants *dge* /j/	145
r-Controlled Vowels: *ear* /er/ and *our* /our/	146-147
Syllable Pattern *tion*	148
Review Long Vowels at the Ends of Syllables	149
Review Consonants *ch* /k/, *sch* /sk/	150

Name _____   Short *a, i, u*

> The letters *a, i,* and *u* stand for short vowel sounds in these words.
>
> cat   pig   bug

Draw a line from each picture to the letter that stands for the short vowel sound in the picture name.

1.
2.

a

3.
4.

i

5.

u

6.
7.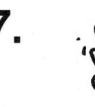

a

8.
9.

i

10.

u

Notes for Home: Your child identified words with the short vowel sounds *a, i,* and *u*.
Home Activity: Challenge your child to name things with the short *a, i,* and *u* vowel sounds and write the words.

Name _____   **Short *a*, *i*, *u***

> Read the words with the short *a*, *i*, and *u* vowel sounds.
>
> c**a**t   p**i**g   b**u**g

Circle the word that completes the sentence. Write the word.

1. I like your _____ and coat.

   hut   hat   hit

   _____

2. Todd has a small _____ on his hand.

   cat   kit   cut

   _____

3. The baby sleeps in a _____.

   crab   crib   cub

   _____

4. Kim has a pet _____.

   duck   dig   dark

   _____

5. Dan turned on the _____.

   limp   lump   lamp

   _____

Notes for Home: Your child wrote words with the short *a*, *i*, and *u* vowel sounds.
Home Activity: Have your child name words for things he or she can find at the grocery store that have a short *a*, *i*, or *u* vowel sound.

Name _____   *l, r,* and *s* Blends

A consonant blend can stand for the beginning sound in a word.

   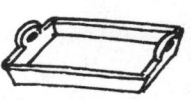 

broom **dr**ill **fl**ute **tr**ay **str**eam

Name the pictures in each row. Circle the pictures whose names have the same beginning consonant blend.

1.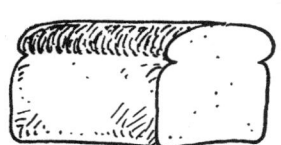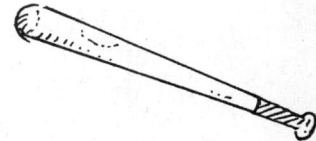

2.

3.

4.

5.

 **Notes for Home:** Your child identified words with the beginning sounds *br, dr, fl, tr,* and *str*.
Home Activity: Have your child draw pictures of things that begin with these consonant blends—*br, dr, fl, tr, str*.

Name _____

Review Initial Consonants
g /j/, *c* /s/

The letter *g* can stand for the sound in *goat* or *gym*.
The letter *c* can stand for the sound in *car* or *cent*.

Circle the pictures that have the same beginning sound.

1.

2.

3.

4.

5.

 **Notes for Home:** Your child reviewed words that begin with the hard and soft *g* and *c* sounds.
Home Activity: Have your child draw pictures of things that can be found in a city and that begin with the hard or soft *g* and the hard or soft *c* sounds.

Name _____   **Review Final Double Consonants**

> Double consonants—*ss, ll,* and *ff*—can stand for the ending sound in words.
>
> pa**ss**   ca**ll**   o**ff**

Write the letters that stand for the ending sound in the picture name.

1.  _____

2.  _____

3. 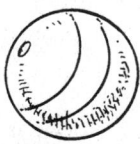 _____

4.  _____

5.  _____

6.  _____

7.  _____

8.  _____

9.  _____

10.  _____

 **Notes for Home:** Your child identified double consonants that stand for the ending sounds in words. **Home Activity:** Help your child write a sentence using two of the words on this page.

5

Name _____ Short *e, o*

The letters *e* and *o* stand for the short vowel sounds in these words.

bed   mop

Circle the word with the same vowel sound as the picture name.

1.		pet cat	2. 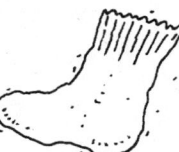	top ten
3.	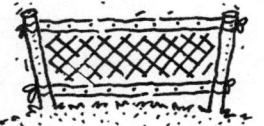	cap red	4. 	sled sock
5.	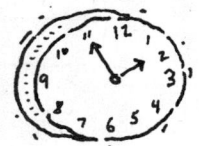	bag pot	6. 	hop pen
7.		cub dock	8. 	nest plum
9.		mom map	10. 	mask desk

Notes for Home: Your child identified words with the short *e* and *o* vowel sounds.
Home Activity: Invite your child to tell a story about a pet using words with the short *e* and *o* vowel sounds.

Name _____ Short *e, o*

> Read the words with the short vowel sounds.
>
> t**e**n   st**o**p

Choose the letter *e* or *o* to finish each word. Write the word.

1. The spider made a w__b.

   _____

2. The door has a l__ck.

   _____

3. The h__n sat on the fence.

   _____

4. The t__p spins fast.

   _____

5. The ball hit the n__t.

   _____

Notes for Home: Your child identified words with the short *e* and *o* vowel sounds.
Home Activity: Read a newspaper or magazine article with your child. Find words with the short *e* or *o* vowel sound.

Name _____   **Final Consonant Blends**

> A consonant blend—*ld, nd, nt, mp,* or *st*—can stand for the ending sound in a word.
>
> go**ld**   wi**nd**   pi**nt**   ca**mp**   mi**st**

Circle the letters that stand for the ending sound in the picture name.

1.  la___ mp / ld
2.  chi___ ld / lt
3.  ne___ ss / st
4.  sta___ nd / mp
5.  ba___ nd / nk
6.  pai___ nd / nt
7.  co___ ld / lt
8.  fi___ sk / st
9.  po___ nt / nd
10.  pla___ ng / nt

Notes for Home: Your child identified consonant blends at the end of words.
Home Activity: Write the letters *ld, nd, nt, mp,* and *st* on a sheet of paper and help your child make a list of other words that end in these letters.

Name _____   Review Consonants *c, k, ck*

> The *k* sound can be spelled with the letters *c, k,* or *ck*.
>
> ba**c**on   la**k**e   sti**ck**

Circle the letters that stand for /k/. Write the word.

1. du●

   c   k   ck

   _____

2. ●ar

   c   k   ck

   _____

3. ●ite

   c   k   ck

   _____

4. ●itten

   c   k   ck

   _____

5. so●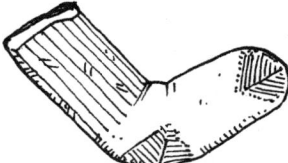

   c   k   ck

   _____

Notes for Home: Your child identified letters that stand for the *k* sound.
Home Activity: Have your child draw a picture of things in a park whose names have the *k* sound and then write *c, k,* or *ck* by each picture.

Name _____   Review *l, r, s* Blends

> These words begin with consonant blends.
> **br**oom   **dr**ess   **fl**ute   **str**eet

Use the word part and the consonant blend *br*, *dr*, *fl*, or *str* to write a word that finishes the phrase.

1.    _____ipe

   a wide _____

2. 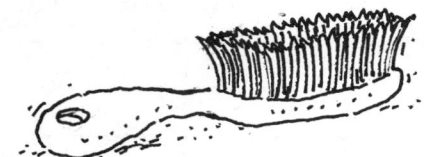   _____ush

   a big _____

3.    _____eam

   a cool _____

4.    _____ower

   a _____ garden

5.    _____ip

   a slow _____

 **Notes for Home:** Your child reviewed words that begin with the consonant blends *br, dr, fl,* and *str*. **Home Activity:** Ask your child to write a riddle about one of the words on this page.

Name _____   Long Vowels with Final *e*

> When a one-syllable word ends in *e*, the vowel sound is long.
>
> cak**e**   min**e**   pol**e**   cut**e**

Circle the word that names the picture.

1.
   plane   plan

2.
   cob   cone

3.
   cub   cube

4.
   fin   five

5.
   rope   rob

6.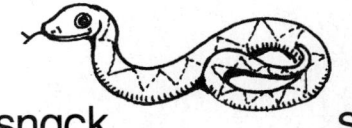
   snack   snake

7.
   mud   mule

8.
   kite   kit

9.
   big   bike

10.
    cane   can

Notes for Home: Your child identified words with long vowel sounds and final *e*.
Home Activity: Have your child make up four sentences using at least one word with a long vowel sound and final *e* in each sentence.

Name _____

Long Vowels with Final *e*

> Words like *cape, bite, zone,* and *mule* have a long vowel sound and final *e*.

Write the word that completes the sentence. The underlined word will rhyme with your answer.

1. The dog tried to <u>bite</u> my _____.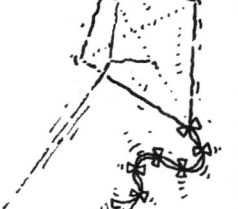

2. "Quizz" is the <u>name</u> of the _____.

3. The <u>mole</u> ran into its _____.

4. A <u>fuse</u> is what Dad will _____.

5. We will <u>bake</u> the _____.

Notes for Home: Your child identified words with long vowel sounds and final *e*.
Home Activity: Encourage your child to write new sentences using the long vowel words on this page.

Name _____   **Initial Consonant Digraphs**

> A consonant digraph—*ch*, *th*, *sh*, or *wh*—can stand for the beginning sound in a word.

Circle the word that names the picture. Then write the word.

1.    corn   _____
   thorn   _____

2.    please   _____
   cheese   _____

3.    shell   _____
   well   _____

4.    crumb   _____
   thumb   _____

5.    tail   _____
   whale   _____

 **Notes for Home:** Your child identified consonant digraphs that stand for beginning sounds in words. **Home Activity:** Have your child make up a tongue twister using words that begin with *ch*, *th*, *sh*, or *wh*.

Name _____   **Review Short Vowels**

The letters *a, e, i, o,* and *u* are vowels that stand for the short vowel sounds in these words.

c**a**b   r**e**d   b**i**g   c**o**t   c**u**t

Circle the picture name. Write the word.

1. wig _____
   wag _____

2. shop _____
   ship _____

3. bag _____
   bug _____

4. nut _____
   net _____

5. fin _____
   fan _____

6. dock _____
   desk _____

7. jog _____
   jug _____

8. rod _____
   red _____

9. pin _____
   pan _____

10. bad _____
    bed _____

Notes for Home: Your child reviewed words with short vowel sounds. **Home Activity:** Have your child think of rhyming words for five of the words on this page.

Name _____

Review Final Consonant Blends

Each of these words ends with a consonant blend.

li**st**   pai**nt**   ba**nd**   co**ld**   ca**mp**

Circle the word to finish the sentence. Write the word.

1. The sun set in the _____.

   west   went

_____

2. Can I _____ the trophy?

   hold   host

_____

3. The pipe was _____.

   best   bent

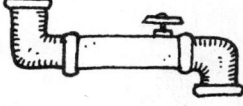

_____

4. The _____ blew hard.

   wild   wind

_____

5. The letter needs a _____.

   stamp   stand

_____

Notes for Home: Your child reviewed words that end with consonant blends *st, nt, nd, mp,* and *ld.* **Home Activity:** Have your child look for a magazine picture whose name ends with a consonant blend and tell a story about the picture.

Name _____ Long *e: ea, ee*

> The long *e* sound can be spelled *ea* and *ee*.
>
> t**ea**m   f**ee**d

Circle the picture in each box that has the long *e* sound.

1.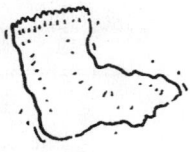
2.
3.
4.
5.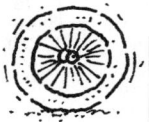
6.
7.
8.
9.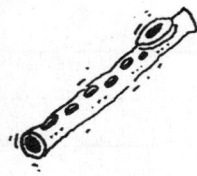
10.

 **Notes for Home:** Your child identified words with the long *e* sound spelled *ea* and *ee*.
Home Activity: Have your child write a short rhyme using words on this page.

Name _____   Long *e: ea, ee*

> The long *e* sound can be spelled *ea* and *ee*.
>
> b**ea**ch   thr**ee**

Look at each picture. Choose a word from the box to complete the sentence. Write the word.

| beans   green   weed   cream   peach |

1. Who will pick a _____?

2. Lin pulled up a _____.

3. The ice _____ is melting.

4. The grass is _____.

5. The _____ are good to eat.

Notes for Home: Your child identified words with the long *e* sound spelled *ea* and *ee*.
Home Activity: Have your child write a silly newspaper headline using words from this page.

17

Name _____   **Final Consonant Digraphs**

> A consonant digraph—*ch, ng, nk, sh,* and *th*—can stand for the ending sound in a word.

Look at the letters. Circle the picture whose name ends with that sound.

1. ch

2. ng

3. nk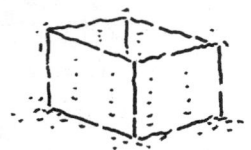

4. sh

5. th

 **Notes for Home:** Your child identified consonant digraphs that stand for ending sounds in words. **Home Activity:** Have your child write sentences using the names for the circled pictures on this page.

Name _____ Review Long Vowels with Final *e*

> Words that end in *e* usually have a long vowel sound.
>
> mate   ride   mule   hose

Circle the word that completes each sentence.

1. I can't find the roll of _____ .   tap   tape

2. Ted went down the _____ in the park.   sled   slide

3. The bear slept in the _____ .   cab   cave

4. The little cub was _____ .   cut   cute

5. There is a _____ in your sweater.   hole   hill

6. An elephant is a _____ animal.   hug   huge

7. Do you _____ to ride your bike?   like   lake

8. The _____ swam in the ocean.   whale   while

9. Put the pan on the _____ .   stop   stove

10. You use your _____ to smell things.   not   nose

Notes for Home: Your child reviewed words with long vowel sounds and final *e*.
Home Activity: Have your child look for magazine pictures whose names have long vowel sounds and final *e*, cut them out, and paste them on a sheet of paper.

Review Initial Consonant Digraphs

Name _____

Say each word and listen to the beginning sound.

chair   **th**umb   **sh**oe   **wh**ale

Write the word that goes with each clue.

cheer   thunder   sheep   whisper   chicken

1. a quiet sound only one person can hear _____

2. makes a noise that sounds like "b-a-a" _____

3. a rumbling sound during a storm _____

4. the sound at a game when your team wins _____

5. makes a cluck, cluck sound _____

Notes for Home: Your child identified consonant digraphs that stand for beginning sounds in words. **Home Activity:** Help your child make a list of words that begin with *ch, th, sh,* and *wh.*

20

Name _____   Long *e: e, y*

> The long *e* sound can be spelled *e* or *y*.
>
> b**e**   bus**y**

Look at each picture. Draw a line from the picture to the word that has the long *e* sound and tells about the picture.

1.    hilly

   road

2.    dog

   silly

3.    girl

   she

4.    bunny

   rabbit

5.   sunshine

   sunny

Notes for Home: Your child identified words that have the long *e* sound spelled *e* and *y*.
Home Activity: Have your child write a story using words that have the long *e* sound spelled *e* and *y*.

Name _____   Long *e: e, y*

> Words like *she* and *silly* have the long *e* sound spelled *e* and *y*.

Write the long *e* word to finish the sentence.

    me   my

1. Uncle Tim sent ____ a present.

_____

    messy   most

2. Nan's room is ____.

_____

    very   vase

3. This tree is ____ tall.

_____

    be   by

4. Ki will ____ late for school.

_____

    funny   first

5. The ____ clown made us laugh.

_____

Notes for Home: Your child identified words that have the long *e* sound spelled *e* and *y*.
Home Activity: Have your child look in magazine or newspaper articles for other words that have the long *e* sound spelled *e* and *y*.

Name _____   **Inflected Ending** *-ed*

The letters *-ed* can be added to the end of some words without changing the spelling of the base word.

paint—paint**ed**   walk—walk**ed**   clean—clean**ed**

Add *-ed* to each word and write the word. Then draw a line to the picture that shows the action.

1. climb _____

2. play _____

3. cook _____

4. yawn _____

5. laugh _____

Notes for Home: Your child identified words that do not change spelling when the ending *-ed* is added. **Home Activity:** Have your child write a sentence using each of the words.

Name _____   Review Long *e: ea, ee*

> The letters *ea* and *ee* can spell the long *e* vowel sound.
>
> dr**ea**m   sp**ee**d

Find words in the box to complete the puzzle.

> meal   sheep   wreath   teeth
> bead   peel   sea   heel

Across
2. circle made of branches
4. skin of an orange
5. body of water

Down
1. lunch or dinner
3. part of your foot

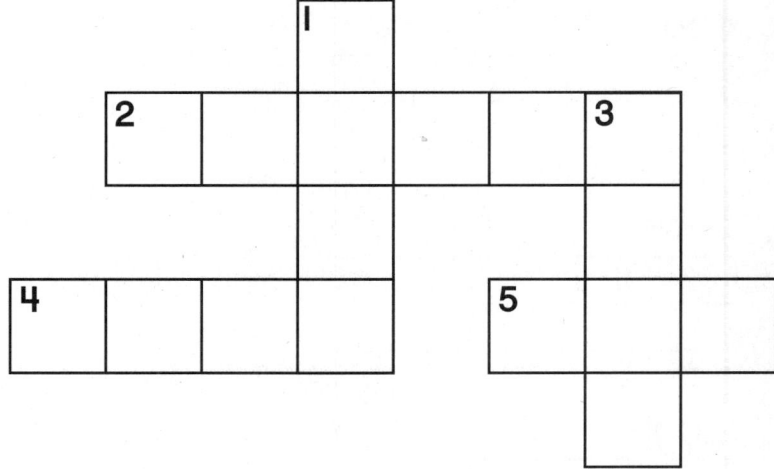

Notes for Home: Your child reviewed words with the long *e* sound spelled *ea* and *ee*.
Home Activity: Have your child write the headings *ee* and *ea* on a sheet of paper and list the words on this page under the correct heading.

24

Name _____

Review Final Consonant Digraphs

The letters *ch, ng, sh,* and *th* stand for the ending sounds in these words.

lun**ch**   ri**ng**   pu**sh**   boo**th**

Find five words in the puzzle that end with *ch, ng, sh,* or *th.* Circle each word in the puzzle. Then write the word.

m	n	v	u	k
s	w	i	n	g
x	q	k	j	p
o	g	w	l	t
y	b	a	t	h
b	t	s	o	i
z	b	h	y	n
d	e	q	i	g
t	o	u	c	h

1. _____
2. _____
3. _____
4. _____
5. _____

Notes for Home: Your child reviewed consonant digraphs that stand for ending sounds in words. **Home Activity:** Have your child write words that end in *ch, ng, sh,* or *th* and then draw a picture to show the meaning of the words.

25

Name _____ Long *a: a, ai, ay*

> The letters *a, ai,* and *ay* can spell the long *a* vowel sound.
>
> t**a**ble   p**ai**l   st**ay**

Circle the word that names each picture and has the long *a* sound.

1.		snow snail	2.	paint pint
3.		he hay	4.	pan paper
5.		ran ray	6.	day dime
7.		track train	8.	bag baby
9.		tray trap	10.	sail seal

Notes for Home: Your child identified words that have the long *a* sound spelled *a, ai,* or *ay*.
Home Activity: Encourage your child to choose five words from this page and use each one in a sentence.

Name _____   Long *a: a, ai, ay*

Words like *paper*, *mail*, and *day* have the long *a* sound spelled *a*, *ai*, and *ay*.

Find a word in the box that rhymes with the underlined word in each sentence. Write the word. Then say the whole rhyme.

| stain | today | table | clay | pail |

1. The cat put its <u>tail</u> in a red _____.

2. This is the <u>way</u> to mold your _____.

3. It's wet and <u>gray</u> outside _____.

4. The <u>rain</u> made a big wet _____.

5. The <u>cable</u> is behind the _____.

Notes for Home: Your child identified words that have the long *a* sound spelled *a*, *ai*, or *ay*.
Home Activity: Have your child write *table*, *rain*, and *way* across the top of a sheet of paper and then find and write words with long *a* sound spelled the same as each word.

Name _____

Inflected Endings
-es, *-ing*, and *-s*

> The letters *-es, -ing,* and *-s* can be added to the end of some words without changing the spelling of the base word.
>
> hatch—hatch**es**   fall—fall**ing**   sit—sit**s**

Add the ending to the new word. Write the new word to finish the phrase.

1. tie   _____ her shoe (**-s**)

2. search   _____ for a lost dog (**-ing**)

3. walk   _____ to school (**-s**)

4. knock   _____ on a door (**-ing**)

5. scratch   _____ an itch (**-es**)

Notes for Home: Your child wrote words that do not change spelling when the ending *-es, -ing,* or *-s* is added. **Home Activity:** Have your child think of words that rhyme with the words from this page and then form new words by adding *-es, -ing,* or *-s*.

Name _____

Review Long e: e, y

The long e sound can be spelled *e* or *y*.

b**e**   hung**ry**

Read the riddles. Write answers that have long *e*.

| open | country | little | we | him |
| tiny | empty | he | farm | us |

1. Where do horses and cows live? _____

2. What size is a mouse? _____

3. What is a box if it has nothing in it? _____

4. What is a word for a friend and me? _____

5. What is a word for a boy? _____

Notes for Home: Your child wrote words that have the long *e* sound spelled *e* and *y*.
Home Activity: Have your child write each word from this page on a card and then take turns with your child drawing a card and using the word in a sentence.

29

Name _____   Review Inflected Ending -ed

> Words like *jump* and *scold* do not change their spelling when -*ed* is added.
>
> jump—jump**ed**   scold—scold**ed**

Underline the word that will correctly complete the sentence when -*ed* is added. Then write the word with -*ed*.

1. Aunt Erica ____ the car.
   sail   wax

   _____

2. We ____ Dad in the yard.
   help   hop

   _____

3. Troy ____ the picture.
   climb   paint

   _____

4. The dog ____ loudly.
   bark   talk

   _____

5. My sisters ____ the garage.
   jump   clean

   _____

Notes for Home: Your child reviewed words that do not change spelling when the ending -*ed* is added. **Home Activity:** Have your child look through a newspaper article and underline other -*ed* words.

Name _____ Long *i*: *i*, *igh*, *y*, *ie*

The long *i* sound can spelled *i*, *igh*, *y*, or *ie*.

iris   l**igh**t   fr**y**   p**ie**

In each row, circle the picture that goes with the word. Then say the word.

1. light

2. night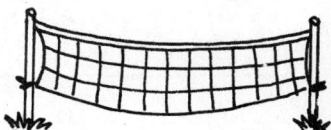

3. fly

4. tie

5. high

 **Notes for Home:** Your child identified words with the long *i* sound spelled *i*, *igh*, *y*, and *ie*.
Home Activity: Have your child write a short poem about the night using some of these words: *high, sky, bright, fly, light, delight.*

Name _____   Long *i: i, igh, y, ie*

The letters *i*, *igh*, *y*, and *ie* can spell the long *i* sound.

    mind   h**igh**   cr**y**   t**ie**

Write each word from the box under the word with the same vowel pattern.

right   find   why   pie   idea

List 1
Words like *mind*

1. _____

2. _____

List 2
Words like *high*

3. _____

List 3
Words like *cry*

4. _____

List 4
Words like *tie*

5. _____

Notes for Home: Your child identified words with the long *i* sound spelled *i*, *igh*, *y*, and *ie*.
Home Activity: Print words that have the long *i* sound on index cards. Have your child pick a card, say the word, and tell the letters that spell long *i*.

32

Name _____   **Medial Consonants**

> Some words have one consonant in the middle: *cabin*.
> Some words have two consonants in the middle: *kitten*.

Say each word. Write the number **1** or **2** to tell how many consonants are in the middle of the word. Then write the words that have two middle consonants.

1. wagon _____
2. follow _____
3. bottom _____
4. tunnel _____
5. metal _____
6. dresser _____
7. pillow _____
8. water _____
9. butter _____
10. lizard _____
11. hippo _____
12. puppy _____
13. tiger _____
14. river _____
15. yogurt _____

Notes for Home: Your child identified words with one and two consonants in the middle.
Home Activity: Have your child write a sentence using each of the animal words from the page.

33

Name _____   Review Long *a*: *a*, *ai*, *ay*

> The letter *a* can stand for the long *a* sound: *paper*.
> The letters *ai* can stand for the long *a* sound: *mail*.
> The letters *ay* can stand for the long *a* sound: *day*.

Read the clue by each picture. Draw a line to the word that tells about the picture and has the long *a* sound.

1. follows an animal      nail

2. a place to eat      home

    spray

3. month for flowers      saw

    water

    tail

4. goes with a hammer      table

    June

5. makes things wet      wagon

    May

 **Notes for Home:** Your child identified words that have the long *a* sound spelled *a*, *ai*, or *ay*. **Home Activity:** Have your child write sentences about a spring day using words like *May*, *jay*, *snail*, *bait*, and *day*.

Name _____

Review Inflected Endings
-es, *-ing*, and *-s*

> Words like *reach*, *bark*, and *sleep* do not change their spelling when *-es*, *-ing*, or *-s* is added.
>
> reach—reach**es**   bark—bark**ing**   sleep—sleep**s**

Unscramble each word and write the correct word.

1. Pedro _____ a letter to a friend.
   estwri

2. Liz looks both ways before she _____ the street.
   ssesorc

3. Sam _____ out the candle.
   swobl

4. The barber _____ Pete's hair.
   tucs

5. Jana is _____ in the parade.
   gnrachim

Notes for Home: Your child identified words that do not change spelling when the ending *-es*, *-ing*, or *-s* is added. **Home Activity:** Have your child add *-es*, *-ing*, and *-s* to the words *push*, *color*, and *talk* to make new words and then write a sentence using each word.

35

Name _____   r-Controlled Vowels: *er, ir, ur*

> The letters *er, ir,* and *ur* stand for the vowel sound in these words.
>
> h**er**   f**ir**st   t**ur**n

Say each picture name. Circle the word that names the picture. Write the word and circle the letters that stand for the vowel-*r* sound.

1.    hut   huge   turtle   _____

2.    dirt   skirt   set   _____

3.   desk   germ   clerk   _____

4.    burn   purse   prune   _____

5.    first   stir   five   _____

 **Notes for Home:** Your child identified the letters that stand for an *r*-controlled vowel sound.
Home Activity: Have your child write a story about one of the pictures.

Name _____ r-Controlled Vowels: *er, ir, ur*

The vowel sound in *perch*, *skirt*, and *nurse* is spelled *er*, *ir*, and *ur*.

Find words in the box to complete the puzzle.

| perk | dirt | serve | perch |
| thirsty | burn | purse | fir |

Across
2. needing a drink of water
5. small bag

Down
1. evergreen tree
3. offer food to
4. bird's resting place

Notes for Home: Your child used words with *r*-controlled vowels to complete a crossword puzzle. **Home Activity:** Have your child cut out magazine pictures whose names contain *r*-controlled vowels *(germs, clerk, herd, dirt, fir, shirt, skirt, bird, burn, fur)*.

Name _____   Plurals -s and -es

To form the plural of many words, add -s. To form the plural of words that end in ch, sh, s, ss, or x, add -es. To form the plural of words that end in a consonant and y, change the y to i before adding -es.

Each picture shows two or more of something. Read the word and write the plural form of the word.

1. letter

2. pony

3. glass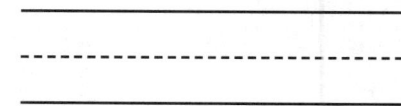

4. fox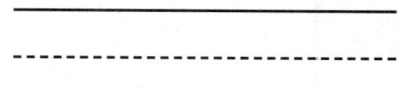

5. puppy

 **Notes for Home:** Your child formed the plural of words by adding -s or -es to the base word.
Home Activity: Have your child look through advertisements and list plural words. Encourage your child to underline the letters that are used to form each plural.

Name _____   **Review Long *i*: *i*, *igh*, *y*, and *ie***

Words like *tiger, sign, try,* and *lie* have the long *i* sound spelled *i, igh, y,* and *ie*.

Name the picture. Write the word with the long *i* sound to complete the phrase.

1.   tie   pit

   a black _____

2.   warm   bright

   the _____ sunshine

3.   dark   high

   a _____ cloud

4.   wild   wet

   a _____ animal

5.   shy   funny

   a _____ student

 **Notes for Home:** Your child identified words with the long *i* sound spelled *i, igh, y,* and *ie*.
Home Activity: Have your child make a list of words in which the long *i* vowel sound is spelled *i, igh, y,* or *ie*.

Name _____   **Review Medial Consonants**

> *Yogurt* and *spider* have one consonant in the middle.
> *Paddle* and *rattle* have double consonants in the middle.

Circle the word that completes the sentence. Write each circled word in the correct list.

1. The ___ slept near the fireplace.   kennel   kitten

2. The dog liked to ride in the ___.   wagon   waffle

3. Drop the ___ in the mailbox.   lever   letter

4. The clown made the girl ___.   gobble   giggle

5. Our ___ is near a lake.   cabin   copper

Double consonants
_____
_____
_____
_____
_____

Single consonants
_____
_____
_____

Notes for Home: Your child identified words with one or two consonants in the middle.
Home Activity: Help your child think of other words with one or two middle consonants and list them on a sheet of paper.

Name _____ Long *o: o, oa, ow, oe*

> The long *o* sound can be spelled with the letters *o, oa, ow,* or *oe*.
>
> **o**nly   fl**oa**t   gr**ow**   h**oe**

Look at each picture. Write the long *o* word for the picture.

1.  _____

2.  _____

3.  _____

4.  _____

5.  _____

6.  _____

7.  _____

8.  _____

9.  _____

10.  _____

Notes for Home: Your child identified words with the long *o* sound spelled *o, oa, ow,* or *oe*.
Home Activity: Have your child write a sentence using four words from this page and draw a picture to go with the sentence.

Name _____ Long *o: o, oa, ow, oe*

The long *o* sound can be spelled with the letters *o*, *oa*, *ow*, or *oe*.

g**o**   t**oa**d   sl**ow**   t**oe**

Write the words that have the long *o* sound inside the giant *o*.

road	low	blow	load
hop	foam	box	clock
goal	top	no	lock
told	fox	only	hoe

Notes for Home: Your child identified words with the long *o* sound spelled *o*, *oa*, *ow*, or *oe*.
Home Activity: Have your child write sentences about a boat trip using the words *boat, float, slow, old,* and *row.*

42

Name _____   **Compound Words**

A compound word is a word made up of two smaller words.

air + plane = airplane   birth + day = birthday

Circle each compound word. Write the compound words.

1. teacher
2. baseball
3. animal
4. afternoon
5. pencil
6. anyone
7. sentence
8. sidewalk
9. outside
10. person
11. doorbell
12. question
13. doghouse
14. notebook
15. tiger

_____ _____ _____

_____ _____ _____

_____ _____

Notes for Home: Your child identified compound words. **Home Activity:** Write the words *down, town, rain, drop, sun, shine, bed, room, every, thing, my,* and *self* on cards and have your child put the cards together to make compound words.

Name _____

Review r-Controlled Vowels:
er, ir, ur

The letters *er, ir,* and *ur* stand for the same vowel sound.

p**er**k   g**ir**l   h**ur**t

Write a word from the box to complete each tongue twister. Then underline the letters that stand for the vowel sound.

| perch | dirt | fir | turn | serve |

1. Sandy will _____ salad in a seashell.   _____

2. Please put Polly Parrot on her _____.   _____

3. Dale's dog Dixie dug deep in the _____.   _____

4. It's Tina's _____ to take a trip.   _____

5. The forest was full of fat _____ trees.   _____

Notes for Home: Your child wrote words with *r*-controlled vowels. **Home Activity:** Help your child look through a book and find words that have the same vowel sound as *girl*.

44

Name _____   **Plurals -s and -es**

> The endings -s and -es are added to words to form the plural. For words that end in a consonant and y, the y is changed to i before -es is added.
>
> jet—jet**s**　　　box—box**es**　　　bench—bench**es**
> wish—wish**es**　　circus—circus**es**　　baby—bab**ies**

Write the word that fits each clue. Then write the plural form of the word.

　　　ocean　　　penny　　　lunch　　　cherry　　　bunny

1. rabbit

2. meal

3. red fruit

4. one cent

5. a whale's home

Notes for Home: Your child formed the plurals of words by adding -s or -es.
Home Activity: Have your child write the words *hand, ax, beach, crash,* and *story* and then write the plural of each word by adding -s or -es.

Name _____   **Words with *ce*, *ge*, *se***

> The letters *ce* and *se* spell the sound at the end of *place* and *house*. The letters *se* can also spell the sound at the end of *please*. The letters *ge* spell the sound at the end of *huge*.

Write a word from the box that makes sense in each phrase.

| page | dance | these | face | mouse |

1. wash your _____

2. _____ shoes

3. a field _____

4. read _____ 354

5. a tap _____

Notes for Home: Your child wrote words that end with the *s, z,* and *j* sounds spelled *ce, se,* and *ge*. **Home Activity:** Have your child make up one sentence using two words that end in *ce* or *se* and another sentence using two words that end in *ge*.

Name _____   Words with *ce, ge, se*

The letters *ce* spell the sound at the end of *place*. The letters *se* spell the sounds at the end of *base* and *please*. The letters *ge* spell the sound at the end of *huge*.

Use the letters *ce*, *ge*, or *se* to finish the word. Then write the word.

 1. pa__

 2. ro__

 3. hou__

 4. fen__

 5. ca__

 6. no__

 7. ra__

 8. ri__

 9. ho__

 10. mou__

 **Notes for Home:** Your child wrote words that end with the *s, z,* and *j* sounds spelled *ce, se,* and *ge*. **Home Activity:** Have your child write a two-line poem using rhyming words such as *cage—page, nose—rose, rice—nice,* or *house—mouse*.

Name _____ **Possessives**

A word that shows ownership ends with a *'s* or *s'*.

teacher—teacher**'s**   teachers—teacher**s'**

Circle the words that describe the picture.

1.    the spider's web

   the spiders web

2.    the babies mother

   the babies' mother

3.    the planes wings

   the plane's wings

4.    the elephant's trunk

   the elephants' trunks

5.    the childrens school

   the children's school

 **Notes for Home:** Your child identified words that show ownership. **Home Activity:** Have your child make a list of things in the house and then write words that tell who the things belong to.

48

Name _____   **Review Long *o*: *o*, *oa*, *ow*, *oe***

> The letters *o*, *oa*, *ow*, and *oe* stand for the long *o* vowel sound.
>
> s**o**   b**oa**t   **ow**n   h**oe**

Write a word from the list to complete each phrase. Then circle the letters that stand for the long *o* sound.

grow	goat	show	goal	float
only	throw	blow	toe	cold

1. _____ a ball

2. scored a _____

3. an _____ child

4. stubbed her _____

5. a _____ winter day

Notes for Home: Your child identified words with the long *o* sound spelled *o*, *oa*, *ow*, or *oe*.
Home Activity: Have your child choose a word from the page and think of a word that rhymes with it.

Name _____   **Compound Words**

Two smaller words put together make a compound word.

side + walk = sidewalk   any + thing = anything

Write the two words that make up each compound word.

1. raincoat = _____ + _____

2. doghouse = _____ + _____

3. mailbox = _____ + _____

4. cookbook = _____ + _____

5. bedroom = _____ + _____

Notes for Home: Your child identified words that make up compound words.
Home Activity: Have your child use each compound word in a sentence.

Name _____   **Vowel Diphthongs *ou*, *ow***

> The letters *ou* stand for the vowel sound in *out*.
> The letters *ow* stand for the vowel sound in *down*.

Circle the word in each row that has the same vowel sound as *out* and *down*.

1.	rope	clock	cow
2.	mouse	pop	soap
3.	frown	cot	rose
4.	hole	cob	found
5.	block	crown	smoke
6.	pound	born	hose
7.	bounce	note	hot
8.	float	ground	mop
9.	dog	lock	south
10.	brown	mom	nose

Notes for Home: Your child identified words with the vowel sound in *out*.
Home Activity: Have your child write four sentences using *ou* and *ow* words from this page.

Name _____   Vowel Diphthongs *ou, ow*

> The letters *ou* and *ow* stand for the vowel sound in *count* and *cow*.

Choose the letters *ou* or *ow* to finish each word. Write the word.

1. We watched the funny cl____n.  _____

2. The s____nd of thunder woke me up.  _____

3. The baby kangaroo hid in the p____ch.  _____

4. The unhappy boy had a fr____n on his face.  _____

5. Use a t____el to dry the dishes.  _____

Notes for Home: Your child wrote *ou* and *ow* words. **Home Activity:** Have your child use *ou* and *ow* words to tell a story about a mouse going to town.

Name _____   **Inflected Endings**

> When a word ends with one vowel followed by one consonant, the final consonant is doubled before *-ed* or *-ing* is added.
>
> drip—dripp**ed**   hug—hugg**ing**

Follow the signs to make a new word. Write the word.

1. trip + ed

2. swim + ing

3. stop + ing

4. run + ing

5. pat + ed

6. mop + ed

7. let + ing

8. shrug + ed

9. hop + ed

10. bat + ing

Notes for Home: Your child doubled the final consonant in words before adding *-ed* and *-ing*.
Home Activity: Have your child write five sentences using words from this page.

Name _____   **Words with *ce, ge, se***

The letters *ce* and *se* spell the sound at the end of *race* and *mouse*. The letters *se* can also spell the sound at the end of *tease*. The letters *ge* spell the sound at the end of *cage*.

Find five words in the puzzle that end with *ce, ge,* or *se*. Circle each word in the puzzle. Then write the word.

```
p   e   f   c   e
l   p   a   g   e
e   t   c   d   h
a   h   e   i   o
s   e   b   s   u
e   g   e   e   s
j   u   i   c   e
```

1. _____

2. _____

3. _____

4. _____

5. _____

Notes for Home: Your child wrote words that end with the *s, z,* and *j* sounds spelled *ce, se,* and *ge*. **Home Activity:** Have your child write two words that end in *ce, se,* or *ge* and then draw a picture to go with each word.

Name _____   **Review Possessives**

> A possessive word ends with *'s* or *s'*.
>
> Betty**'s** book   the girl**s'** shoes

Add *'s* or *s'* to the underlined word to show ownership.

1. the desks of the <u>students</u>

   _____

   the _____ desks

2. the book of <u>Miguel</u>

   _____

   _____ book

3. the buttons of the <u>shirt</u>

   _____

   the _____ buttons

4. the playground of the <u>school</u>

   _____

   the _____ playground

5. the uniforms of the <u>players</u>

   _____

   the _____ uniforms

Notes for Home: Your child added *'s* or *s'* to words to show ownership.
Home Activity: Write the names of familiar people and objects on one side of cards and have your child write the possessive forms of the words on the other side.

Name _____   r-Controlled Vowel: *ar*

> The letters *ar* stand for the vowel sound in *card*.

Circle the word that completes each sentence and has the same vowel sound as *card*. Write the word.

1. The kitten plays with _____.
   yarn   me
   _____

2. Uncle Lin bought a new _____.
   bike   car
   _____

3. We saw a _____ in the ocean.
   shark   whale
   _____

4. The band will _____ .
   play   march
   _____

5. Put the marbles in a _____.
   jar   sack
   _____

Notes for Home: Your child wrote *ar* words to complete sentences. **Home Activity:** Have your child write a sentence for each *ar* word on the page.

Name _____   r-Controlled Vowel: *ar*

> The letters *ar* stand for the vowel sound in *car*.

Write the *ar* word that means the opposite of each word.

| part | hard | start | far | dark |

1. finish   _____

2. near   _____

3. light   _____

4. whole   _____

5. soft   _____

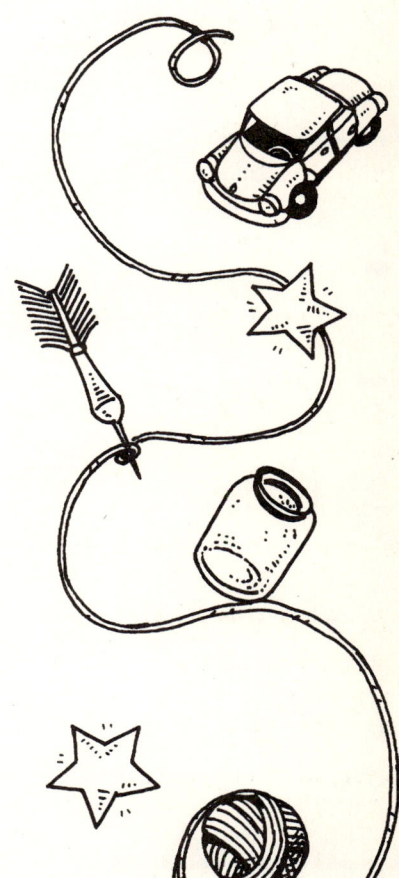

Notes for Home: Your child wrote *ar* words. **Home Activity:** Have your child look for magazine pictures of objects whose names have the same vowel sound as *car*.

57

Name _____   **Inflected Endings**

> When a word ends with *e*, the *e* is dropped before *-ed* or *-ing* is added.
>
> smile—smil**ed**   ride—rid**ing**

Choose the word that makes sense in the sentence. Add the ending and write the word.

1. My cousin is _____ to Ohio. (**-ing**)
   move   judge

2. I _____ the book I read. (**-ed**)
   like   time

3. Uncle Rio _____ a loaf of bread. (**-ed**)
   bake   rake

4. The runners _____ around the track. (**-ed**)
   trace   race

5. Claire is _____ a letter to her pen pal. (**-ing**)
   care   write

Notes for Home: Your child dropped the final *e* in words before adding *-ed* and *-ing*.
Home Activity: Take turns with your child choosing a word from the page and telling what it means.

Name _____

Review Vowel Diphthongs
ou, ow

> The letters *ou* and *ow* stand for the vowel sound in the words *count* and *cow*.

Write the word that goes with the other words in each group and has the vowel sound in *cow*.

south	brown	north	flower	sponge
farm	towel	owl	juggler	sofa
hawk	rat	blue	couch	town
mouse	grass	crown	queen	clown

1. bath, soap, _____

2. tree, plant, _____

3. east, west, _____

4. squirrel, rabbit, _____

5. eagle, robin, _____

6. castle, king, _____

7. chair, stool, _____

8. acrobat, ringmaster, _____

9. city, village, _____

10. red, green, _____

Notes for Home: Your child identified *ou* and *ow* words. **Home Activity:** Have your child find two words on this page that rhyme and write a riddle using them.

Name _____   **Inflected Endings**

> Some words double the final consonant when -ed and -ing are added.
>
> clap—clap**ped**—clap**ping**

Each number stands for a letter of the alphabet. Use the code to write each word. Then add -ed and -ing to the word.

1	2	3	4	5	6	7	8	9	10	11	12	13
a	b	d	h	g	i	l	m	p	r	s	t	u

Code word   **with -ed**   **with -ing**

1. 3 + 6 + 9

2. 4 + 13 + 5

3. 11 + 7 + 1 + 8

4. 5 + 10 + 1 + 2

5. 12 + 10 + 6 + 9

Notes for Home: Your child doubled the final consonant in words before adding -ed and -ing.
Home Activity: Have your child add -ed and -ing to *tap*, *sip*, and *tip*.

Name _____

Sound of Vowel Patterns
ew, oo, ou

> The letters *ew, oo,* and *ou* can spell the same vowel sound.
>
> dr**ew**   r**oo**m   y**ou**

Circle the word that names each picture. Then write the circled word in the correct column.

1.    soup / loop

2.    zoom / moon

3.    knew / grew

4. 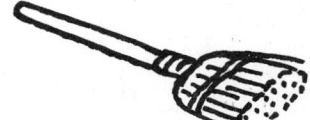   broom / boom

5.    blew / crew

---

Vowel sound spelled *ew*
_____
_____

Vowel sound spelled *oo*
_____
_____

Vowel sound spelled *ou*
_____
_____

Notes for Home: Your child identified words with the vowel patterns *ew, oo,* and *ou*.
Home Activity: Read the circled words together and make up sentences for the words.

61

Sound of Vowel Patterns
ew, oo, ou

The letters *ew, oo,* and *ou* can spell the same vowel sound.

bl**ew**   l**oo**p   gr**ou**p

Follow the directions in each sentence. Use words from the list.

drew   cool   goose   grew   soup

1. Write the word that rhymes with *pool*. Circle the way the vowel sound is spelled.

2. Write the word that rhymes with *new*. Circle the way the vowel sound is spelled.

3. Write the word for a large bird. Circle the way the vowel sound is spelled.

4. Write the word that rhymes with *group*. Circle the way the vowel sound is spelled.

5. Write the word for what an artist did. Circle the way the vowel sound is spelled.

Notes for Home: Your child identified words with the vowel patterns *ew, oo,* and *ou*.
Home Activity: Have your child make up a story using the words *flew, cool, ooze, grew,* and *balloon*.

Name _____   Contractions

> A contraction is a shorter way of writing two words. An apostrophe takes the place of the letter or letters that are left out.

Circle the words that are used to make the contraction.

1. wasn't	was not were not would not	2. you'll	you are you will you were
3. they're	they will they would they are	4. he's	he was he is he will
5. we've	we were we will we have	6. didn't	do not did not has not

Use one of the contractions above to complete each sentence.

7. Eric says _____ going home.

8. Nita _____ at school today.

9. I know _____ like the movie.

10. We _____ see Shawna there.

Notes for Home: Your child identified words used in contractions. **Home Activity:** Have your child look through a magazine or newspaper article and underline contractions.

63

Name _____   Review *r*-Controlled Vowel: *ar*

> The letters *ar* stand for the vowel sound in these words.
>
> p**ar**t   b**ar**n   m**ar**ch

Use the words in the box to complete the puzzle.

| star | carve | yard | scarf | smart |

Across
1. clever
3. cut into slices
4. Let's play in the ___.

Down
1. shines in the sky
2. You wear it around your neck.

Notes for Home: Your child used words with the *ar* vowel sound to complete the puzzle.
Home Activity: Work with your child to list other words with the *ar* vowel sound.

Name _____   **Inflected Endings**

When a word ends in *e*, the *e* is dropped before *-ed* or *-ing* is added.

　　　　　car**e**—car**ed**　　　hik**e**—hik**ing**

Write each word. Then write the word with *-ed* and *-ing*.

| rake | smile | trace | like | skate |

Word　　　　　　**Add -ed**　　　　　　**Add -ing**

1. _____　_____　_____

2. _____　_____　_____

3. _____　_____　_____

4. _____　_____　_____

5. _____　_____　_____

Notes for Home: Your child dropped the final *e* in words before adding *-ed* and *-ing*.
Home Activity: Look through a newspaper together to find words that follow this pattern. Make a list of the words.

Name _____

r-Controlled Vowels:
or, ore, oor, our

Read the words and listen for the vowel sound.

h**or**n   m**ore**   fl**oor**   f**our**

Write the *r*-controlled vowel word used in each sentence.

1. She will pour the water. _____

2. It is cooler on the porch. _____

3. Joel knocked on the front door. _____

4. The score of the game was 6 to 3. _____

5. The horse ran through the meadow. _____

Notes for Home: Your child identified words with the *or, ore, oor,* and *our* vowel patterns.
Home Activity: Write the letters *or, ore, oor,* and *our* on paper and help your child write other words with these vowel patterns.

Name _____

r-Controlled Vowels:
or, ore, oor, our

> The letters *or, ore, oor,* and *our* stand for the vowel sound in these words.
>
>   c**or**n   t**ore**   d**oor**   f**our**

Write the word that answers the question. Draw a line under the letters that stand for the vowel sound.

1. Do you blow a cork or a horn?   _____

2. Is ten more or less than six?   _____

3. Do you sit on t he door or the floor?   _____

4. Is a storm or a stork a bird?   _____

5. Do you core or pour a glass of milk?   _____

Notes for Home: Your child wrote words with the *or, ore, oor,* and *our* vowel patterns.
Home Activity: Help your child write questions using these vowel-*r* words: *porch, before, court.*

Name _____   Inflected Endings

> If the base word ends in *y*, the *y* is changed to *i* before *-ed* or *-es* is added.
> If the base word ends in *y*, the *y* stays when *-ing* is added.
>
> carry—carr**ies**—carr**ied**—carr**ying**

Write each word from the box under the heading that tells what happens to the base word when *-ed*, *-es*, or *-ing* is added.

| hurries | crying | dried | worrying | tries |
| fried | trying | prying | drying | supplied |

No change

1. _____
2. _____
3. _____
4. _____
5. _____

Change *y* to *i*

6. _____
7. _____
8. _____
9. _____
10. _____

Notes for Home: Your child identified words in which the spelling changes before *-ed* or *-es* is added. **Home Activity:** Have your child write the base words for the words on this page.

Name _____

Review Sound of Vowel Patterns
ew, oo, ou

The letters *ew, oo,* and *ou* can spell the same vowel sound.

n**ew**   z**oo**m   gr**ou**p

Write the word that matches each clue. Draw a line under the letters that stand for the vowel sound in the word.

| you | soup | stool | drew | spoons |

1. food made by boiling vegetables or meat _____

2. eating tools _____

3. something to sit on _____

4. made a picture _____

5. the person spoken to _____

Notes for Home: Your child wrote words with the vowel patterns *ew, oo,* and *ou*.
Home Activity: Help your child write a rhyming word for each word on this page.

69

Name _____   **Contractions**

> An apostrophe (') takes the place of the letter or letters that are left out when two smaller words are written as a contraction.
>
> do not—don't

Write the contraction for the underlined words in each sentence.

1. Leah says <u>she is</u> going home. _____

2. <u>You are</u> late for dinner. _____

3. <u>We have</u> been playing basketball. _____

4. Iyo <u>did not</u> water the plants. _____

5. <u>I will</u> meet you at the library. _____

Notes for Home: Your child has written two smaller words as contractions.
Home Activity: Help your child make a list of contractions.

Name _____   **Sound of Vowel Patterns *oo, ou***

> The letters *oo* and *ou* stand for the same vowel sound in these words.
>
> l**oo**k   c**ou**ld

Circle each word that has the same vowel sound as the picture name.

cook

woods   soup

should   hood   shook

took   goat   would   count

stood   too   good   though

brook   couldn't   found

moon   bounce

Notes for Home: Your child identified words with the vowel patterns *oo* and *ou*.
Home Activity: Help your child write a paragraph using the words *cook, shook, took,* and *book*.

Name _____   **Sound of Vowel Patterns** *oo, ou*

> The letters *oo* and *ou* stand for the vowel sound in these words.
>
> **too**k   **cou**ld

Write the word that has the same vowel sound as the first word in the row.

hood   1. school   book   room   _____

should 2. around   couldn't   dough   _____

cook   3. woods   zoom   tooth   _____

good   4. wouldn't you   tool   _____

foot   5. flour   brook   pool   _____

Notes for Home: Your child identified words with the vowel patterns *oo* and *ou*.
Home Activity: Have your child write a book title using one word with the *oo* vowel pattern and one word with the *ou* vowel pattern.

Name _____ Comparative Endings *-er, -est*

> To compare two things, *-er* is added to the base word.
> To compare three or more things, *-est* is added to the base word.
>
> big—bigg**er** than you   little—littl**est** of all

Add *-er* or *-est* to the base word to complete each phrase.

1. **wise** _____ than an owl

2. **fat** _____ of all the puppies

3. **hot** _____ than last summer

4. **tall** _____ of the buildings

5. **large** _____ house on the street

Notes for Home: Your child used words with *-er* and *-est* endings to make comparisons.
Home Activity: Have your child gather household objects and compare them using *little, new,* and *big* with *-er* and *-est* endings.

Name _____

Review r-Controlled Vowels:
or, ore, oor, our

The letters *or, ore, oor,* and *our* stand for the vowel sound in these words.

cor**n**   **s**ore   **d**oor   **p**our

Write each word in the correct box.

| horn | before | court | pork | born |
| four | floor | tore | north | more |

or
1. _____
2. _____
3. _____
4. _____

ore
6. _____
7. _____
8. _____

oor
5. _____

our
9. _____
10. _____

Notes for Home: Your child wrote words with the *r*-controlled vowels *or, ore, oor,* and *our*.
Home Activity: Have your child choose five words from this page and write a sentence using each word.

Name _____   **Inflected Endings**

> The *y* is changed to *i* before *-es* and *-ed* is added if the base word ends in *y*.
> The *y* is kept when *-ing* is added if the base word ends in *y*.
>
> **dry   dries   dried   drying**

Add *-ed* to each word. Write the word.

1. try _____   2. pry _____

3. marry _____   4. reply _____

Add *-es* to each word. Write the word.

5. fry _____   6. cry _____

7. carry _____   8. worry _____

Add *-ing* to each word. Write the word.

9. fly _____   10. hurry _____

Notes for Home: Your child changed the spelling of base words before adding *-ed* or *-es*.
Home Activity: Have your child choose four words from this page and write a sentence using each one.

Name _____   r-Controlled Vowels: *ear, eer*

> The letters *ear* and *eer* stand for the vowel sound in these words.
>
> n**ear**   d**eer**

Underline the words in the box that have the same vowel sound as *near* and *deer*. Then write each underlined word next to its meaning.

clear	read	break	year	beard
cheer	leather	head	steer	great

1. twelve months _____

2. grows on the chin _____

3. an animal _____

4. shout or yell _____

5. can see through _____

Notes for Home: Your child identified words with the *r*-controlled vowels *ear* and *eer*.
Home Activity: Work together with your child and make up sentences using the words he or she wrote.

76

Name _____ r-Controlled Vowels: *ear, eer*

> The letters *ear* and *eer* stand for the vowel sound in these words.
>
> d**ear**　　st**ee**r

Choose a word to finish the sentence that has the vowel sound in *dear* and *steer*. Write the word. Then circle the letters that spell the vowel sound.

1.  We used _____ tape to seal it.
   clear　　sticky

2.  The shed is _____ the trees.
   by　　near

3.  The crowd _____ for the team.
   cheers　　yells

4.  I didn't _____ the bell ring.
   make　　hear

5.  A _____ ran across the road.
   deer　　doe

Notes for Home: Your child identified words with the *r*-controlled vowels *ear* and *eer*.
Home Activity: Help your child make a list of other words with this vowel sound.

Name _____   Suffix -*ly*

> When the suffix -*ly* is added to a base word, it makes a new word that tells how something is done. If the base word ends in *y*, the *y* is changed to *i* before -*ly* is added.
>
> swift—swift**ly**   happy—happ**ily**

Add -*ly* to the base word to make a new word. Then use each new word to complete a sentence. Some words may work in more than one sentence.

1. bright _____
2. quiet _____
3. slow _____
4. loud _____
5. busy _____
6. Speak _____ when you are in a library.
7. The snail _____ crawled through the garden.
8. The airplane roared _____ overhead.
9. We were _____ decorating the room.
10. The candle shines _____.

Notes for Home: Your child added the suffix -*ly* to base words.
Home Activity: Challenge your child to think of words that describe the following actions: *dressed, stirred, slept, sang, played.*

Name _____   **Sound of Vowel Patterns *oo*, *ou***

The letters *oo* and *ou* stand for the vowel sound in these words.

h**oo**d   w**ou**ld

Choose a word to complete each sentence. Circle the letters that spell the vowel sound.

1. We sailed little boats in the _____ .
   brook   book

2. I think that is a _____ idea.
   good   wood

3. _____ you help me with my homework?
   Cook   Could

4. I _____ hands with the mayor.
   should   shook

5. Sam _____ the bus to school.
   look   took

Notes for Home: Your child wrote words with the vowel patterns *oo* and *ou*.
Home Activity: Have your child identify rhyming words from this page.

Name _____   **Comparative Endings** -*er*, -*est*

> The endings -*er* and -*est* are added to a base word to compare things.
>
> small**er** than a ladybug   the litt**lest** flower in the garden

Choose the best word to complete the sentence. Add -*er* or -*est* and write the new word.

1. This line is _____ than that one.
   long   clean

2. The white kitten is the _____ one of all.
   cute   dark

3. A turtle is _____ than a rabbit.
   slow   fast

4. My pillow is _____ than yours.
   wet   soft

5. A pencil is _____ than a book.
   fat   thin

Notes for Home: Your child used words with -*er* and -*est* endings to make comparisons.
Home Activity: Have your child cut out a magazine picture and write a sentence about the picture using -*er* or -*est* to make a comparison.

Name _____ **Vowel Diphthongs** *oi, oy*

> The letters *oi* and *oy* stand for the vowel sound in these words.
>
> **boil**   **joy**

Circle each word that has the same vowel sound as the picture name.

1.

join	phone	pint	dime
choose	toy	chin	road
tiny	point	try	rid
joy	dirt	voice	royal

Write one of the circled words to complete each phrase. You will not use all the words.

2. the pencil's sharp _____

3. a loud _____

4. the baby's favorite _____

5. _____ the team

Notes for Home: Your child wrote words with the vowel diphthongs *oi* and *oy*.
Home Activity: Work with your child to make up meaning clues for *noise, foil, loyal,* and *destroy*.

Name _____   **Vowel Diphthongs *oi*, *oy***

The letters *oi* and *oy* stand for the vowel sound in *join* and *royal*.

Circle the *oi* or *oy* word that completes each sentence. Write the word.

1. Sam put the ___ in his bank.
   coin
   oil
   _____

2. Did you hear a loud ___?
   choice
   noise
   _____

3. The ___ ran in the race.
   toy
   boy
   _____

4. Do you ___ playing ball?
   annoy
   enjoy
   _____

5. Our garden has rich ___.
   soil
   joint
   _____

Notes for Home: Your child wrote words with the vowel diphthongs *oi* and *oy*.
Home Activity: Have your child read the five words that were *not* circled on the page and make up a sentence using each one.

Name _____   Suffix -*ful*

> The suffix -*ful* can be added to a base word.
>
> forget + ful = forget**ful**

Add -*ful* to each base word. Write the new word.

1. color _____
2. care _____
3. harm _____
4. power _____
5. peace _____
6. grace _____
7. play _____
8. hope _____
9. help _____
10. cheer _____

Notes for Home: Your child added the suffix -*ful* to base words. **Home Activity:** Take turns with your child choosing a -*ful* word from the page and making up a silly sentence using the word.

Name _____

Review r-Controlled Vowels: ear, eer

> The letters *ear* and *eer* stand for the vowel sound in *fear* and *deer*.

Use the code to write each word. Then read the letter.

1	2	3	4	5	6	7	8	9
a	d	e	g	h	n	r	s	y

Dear Rusty,

Sam and I go camping every (1.) _____.
$\qquad\qquad\qquad\qquad\qquad\qquad\qquad\quad 9 + 3 + 1 + 7$

We put our (2.) _____ in the car.
$\qquad\qquad\quad 4 + 3 + 1 + 7$

We drive to a camp (3.) _____ a stream.
$\qquad\qquad\qquad\qquad\quad 6 + 3 + 1 + 7$

We hike along (4.) _____ rock cliffs.
$\qquad\qquad\qquad 8 + 5 + 3 + 3 + 7$

We see (5.) _____ as we hike.
$\qquad\qquad 2 + 3 + 3 + 7$

$\qquad\qquad\qquad\qquad\qquad$ Your friend,

$\qquad\qquad\qquad\qquad\qquad$ Mari

Notes for Home: Your child wrote words with the *r*-controlled vowels *ear* and *eer*.
Home Activity: Help your child use the words on the page to write two-line rhymes.

Name _____ Review Suffix -*ly*

> The suffix -*ly* can be added to a base word to make a new word.
>
> quick—quick**ly**   pretty—prett**ily**

Choose a word from the box to answer each clue. Add -*ly* to the base word and write the word. Some words can answer more than one clue.

| swift | quiet | sad | happy | slow |

1. how the children played in the park _____

2. how a fox runs _____

3. how the boy spoke in the library _____

4. how the girl looked at her broken doll _____

5. how a turtle moves _____

Notes for Home: Your child added the suffix -*ly* to base words. **Home Activity:** Have your child choose three -*ly* words from the page and write a sentence for each word.

Name _____   Short *e: ea*

> The word *ready* has the short *e* sound spelled with the letters *ea*.

Say the two picture names. Write the word that has the short *e* vowel sound spelled *ea* as in *ready*.

1.   _____

2.   _____

3.   _____

4.   _____

5.   _____

Notes for Home: Your child identified words with the short *e* vowel sound spelled *ea*.
Home Activity: Together make up a sentence for each picture name with the short *e* vowel sound.

Name _____   **Short *e*: *ea***

> The short *e* sound can be spelled *ea*.

Underline the words with the same vowel sound as *ready*. Then follow the directions.

treasure	great	dead	steak	wealth
breakfast	weather	break	bread	head
real	sweater	leave	heavy	meadow

1. Write the word that names a meal. _____

2. Write the word that rhymes with *feather*. _____

3. Write the word that means a great deal of money. _____

4. Write the word that names something to eat. _____

5. Write the word that names part of the body. _____

Notes for Home: Your child identified words with the short *e* vowel sound spelled *ea*.
Home Activity: Look through a newspaper together to find words with short *e* spelled *ea*.

87

Name _____   **Suffix** *-er*

> When you add the suffix *-er* to a word, you make a new word that means a person or thing that does something.
>
> bake—bak**er**   jog—jog**ger**

Add *-er* to the word that tells about the picture. Write the new word.

1.  play
   paint
   _____

2.  help
   farm
   _____

3.  work
   dance
   _____

4.  skate
   run
   _____

5.  mix
   clean
   _____

Notes for Home: Your child added the suffix *-er* to make new words.
Home Activity: Together add *-er* to the other words on the page.

Name _____   **Review Vowel Diphthongs** *oi, oy*

> The letters *oi* and *oy* stand for the vowel sound in the words *foil* and *toy*.

Choose a word from the box that can replace the underlined word or words in each sentence. Write the word.

| moist | boil | boy | joy | soil |

1. We planted seeds in the <u>dirt</u>. _____

2. Saad washed his face with a <u>wet</u> cloth. _____

3. The <u>young man</u> rode his bike to school. _____

4. The water in the pot began to <u>cook rapidly</u>. _____

5. Her heart was filled with <u>happiness</u>. _____

Notes for Home: Your child wrote words with the vowel diphthongs *oi* and *oy*.
Home Activity: Have your child choose two words from the page and write a riddle about each word.

89

Name _____   Review Suffix -*ful*

> The suffix -*ful* can be added to a base word to make a new word.
>
> cheer + ful = cheer**ful**

Circle the word that completes each phrase when -*ful* is added. Add -*ful* to the word and write the new word.

1. a ___ present   wonder   _____

   hope   _____

2. a ___ quilt   care   _____

   color   _____

3. a ___ kitten   help   _____

   play   _____

4. a ___ insect   harm   _____

   hope   _____

5. the ___ dancer   grace   _____

   harm   _____

Notes for Home: Your child added the suffix -*ful* to base words. **Home Activity:** Challenge your child to add -*ful* and write phrases for words that were *not* circled on the page.

Name _____ /ȯ/ **Vowel Patterns a, al, au**

> The letters *a, al,* and *au* stand for the vowel sound in these words.
>
> water   false   cause

Follow the directions. Use words from the list.

fall   pause   salt   small   fault

1. Write the word for the time after *summer*. Circle the letters that stand for the vowel sound. _____

2. Write the word that means the same as *mistake*. Circle the letters that stand for the vowel sound. _____

3. Write the word that means the opposite of *large*. Circle the letters that stand for the vowel sound. _____

4. Write the word that goes with *pepper*. Circle the letters that stand for the vowel sound. _____

5. Write the word that means "to stop for a time." Circle the letters that stand for the vowel sound. _____

Notes for Home: Your child identified words with the vowel patterns *a, al,* and *au*.
Home Activity: Have your child make up a sentence for each word he or she wrote.

91

Name _____

/ȯ/ **Vowel Patterns a, al, au**

> The words *water*, *walk*, and *cause* have the same vowel sound.
>
> w**a**ter   w**al**k   c**au**se

Circle the word that tells about the picture. Write the word.

1. stalk   saucer
   _____
   _____

2. 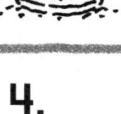 false   laundry
   _____
   _____

3.  salt   small
   _____
   _____

4.  call   cause
   _____
   _____

5.  water   walk
   _____
   _____

6.  ball   fault
   _____
   _____

7.  false   talk
   _____
   _____

8.  faucet   laundry
   _____
   _____

9.  tall   small
   _____
   _____

10.  hall   walnut
    _____
    _____

Notes for Home: Your child identified words with the vowel patterns *a, al,* and *au*.
Home Activity: Help your child make up meaning clues for the circled words on the page.

Name _____   Silent Letters: *kn, mb*

> Some words have letters that are silent.
> When you say *know,* you do not hear the *k.*
> When you say *climb,* you do not hear the *b.*

Circle the letter that you do not hear.

1.  thumb
2. knit
3.  lamb
4.  knife
5.  comb
6.  knee
7.  climb
8.  knuckles
9.  crumbs
10.  knot

Notes for Home: Your child identified words with silent letters. **Home Activity:** Have your child make up riddles using three words from the page.

Name _____   **Review Short *e*: *ea***

> The letters *ea* stand for the vowel sound in the words *wealth* and *head*.

Follow each direction. Write the word.

1. Write *feather*. Circle the letters that spell the short *e* sound.

2. Change the *f* to *l* and write the new word.

3. Change the *l* to *w* and write the new word.

4. Write *thread*. Circle the letters that spell the short *e* sound.

5. Change *th* to *sp* and write the new word.

Notes for Home: Your child wrote words with the short *e* sound spelled *ea*.
Home Activity: Start with the word *threat*. Change, add, or subtract letters to make new words.

Name _____   Review Suffix *-er*

> Adding *-er* to a base word makes a new word that tells who does the action.
>
> A walk**er** is a person who walks.
> A paint**er** is a person who paints.

Directions: Add *-er* to the base word to make a new word that tells who does the action.

1. climb _____   2. drum _____

3. sing _____   4. bake _____

5. hunt _____   6. swim _____

7. run _____   8. manage _____

9. bike _____   10. print _____

Notes for Home: Your child added *-er* to base words to make new words.
Home Activity: Look for *-er* words in the job section of a newspaper. Read the words together and tell what the words mean.

Name _____   /ô/ **Vowel Patterns *aw, ough***

> The letters *aw* and *ough* stand for the vowel sound in these words.
>
> jaw   bought

Choose a word from the box that has the same vowel sound as *jaw* and *bought* and makes sense in the sentence. Write the word.

| thought | doze | dawn | did | eight |
| grass | yawn | said | lawn | saw |

1. Jenna woke up before ___. _____

2. She went outside to mow the ___. _____

3. She was so tired that she began to ___. _____

4. She ___ she would take a little nap. _____

5. Can you guess what Tom ___? _____

Notes for Home: Your child identified words with the vowel patterns *aw* and o*ugh*.
Home Activity: Have your child read the words he or she wrote and make up a sentence for each one.

Name _____ /ô/ **Vowel Patterns** *aw, ough*

> The vowel sound in law and thought is spelled *aw* and *ough*.

Read the word at the beginning of each row. Circle the word that has the same vowel sound.

cough	1.	brought	couch	coach
crawl	2.	spare	few	hawk
straw	3.	fawn	dart	chair
lawn	4.	lane	sought	careful
fought	5.	fowl	soup	bought
draw	6.	star	dawn	mare
thaw	7.	ought	rare	want
dawn	8.	down	jaw	far
bought	9.	should	group	yawn
ought	10.	raw	tough	door

Notes for Home: Your child identified words with the vowel patterns *aw* and *ough*.
Home Activity: Challenge your child to tell a story using the words *crawl, hawk, fawn, saw, straw, lawn,* and *thaw*.

Name _____ **Silent Letters:** *gn, wh, wr*

Sometimes two letters together stand for only one sound.

The *gn* in *sign* stands for the *n* sound.
The *wh* in *who* stands for the *h* sound.
The *wr* in *wring* stands for the *r* sound.

Circle the letters that complete the word. Then write the word.

1. a strong __ __ estler   [ART: wrestler]   _____

   gn   wr   wh

2. a bold desi __ __   [ART: a geometric design]   _____

   gn   wr   wh

3. a __ __ ole pizza   [ART: a pizza]   _____

   gn   wr   wh

4. a __ __ at bite   [ART: a gnat]   _____

   gn   wr   wh

5. the boy's __ __ ist   [ART: arm, arrow to wrist]   _____

   gn   wr   wh

Notes for Home: Your child identified words with silent letters. **Home Activity:** Have your child choose three of the phrases above and rewrite them as sentences.

Name _____

**Review /ȯ/
Vowel Patterns *a*, *al*, *au***

In the words *water*, *talk*, and *taught*, the letters *a*, *al*, and *au* stand for the vowel sound.

Write the words from the box to complete the puzzle.

| walk | faucet | false | water | saucer |

Across
2. turns water on and off
4. holds a cup

Down
1. something to drink
2. not true
3. move around

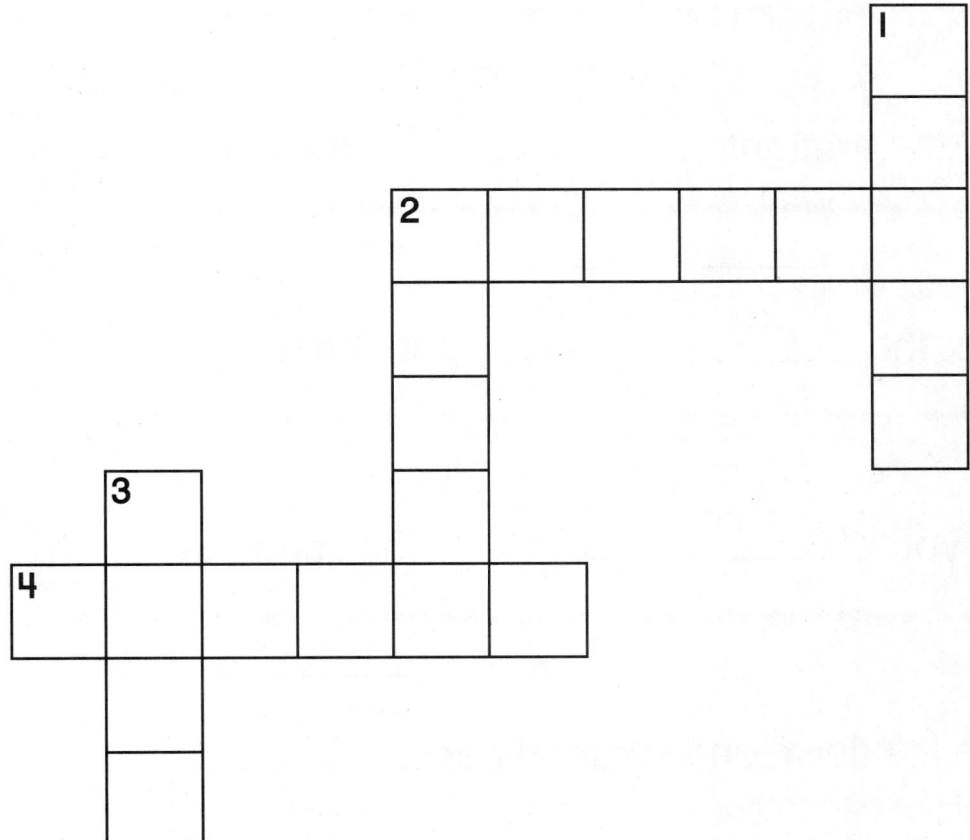

Notes for Home: Your child used words with the vowel patterns *a*, *al*, and *au* to complete a puzzle. **Home Activity:** Write the headings *a*, *al*, and *au* on paper and together with your child think of words to write under each heading.

99

Name _____

Review Silent Letters: *kn, mb*

Sometimes words have letters that are silent.

The *b* in *limb* is silent.
The *k* in *knife* is silent.

Write a word from the box to complete each sentence. Then circle the letter that is silent.

| knob | know | climb | thumb | knee |

1. The baby sucked his _____ .

2. Will the firefighter _____ the ladder?

3. Turn the _____ to open the door.

4. Do you _____ where the library is?

5. She fell down and scraped her _____ .

Notes for Home: Your child wrote words with silent letters. **Home Activity:** Work together with your child to list other words with silent letters.

Name _____   **Short *u*: *ou***

> The short *u* sound can be spelled *ou* as in *young*.

Write the word that tells about the picture. Circle the letters that spell the short *u* sound.

1.  country _____
   young _____

2.  enough _____
   couple _____

3.  touch _____
   double _____

4. 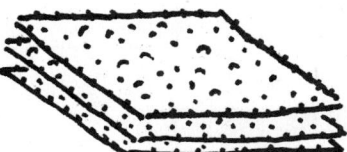 cousin _____
   rough _____

5.  double _____
   southern _____

Notes for Home: Your child wrote words with the short *u* sound spelled *ou*.
Home Activity: Have your child write sentences using five words from this page.

Name _____   **Short *u*: *ou***

> In words like *rough* and *cousin*, the letters *ou* stand for the short *u* vowel sound.

Choose a word from the list to complete each sentence. Write the word and circle the letters that stand for the short *u* sound.

southern   enough   touch   country   young

1. We saw cows and sheep in the ___.   _____

2. Georgia is a ___ state.   _____

3. Don't ___ the hot stove!   _____

4. There aren't ___ seats for everyone.   _____

5. My brother is too ___ to go to school.   _____

Notes for Home: Your child wrote words with the short *u* sound spelled *ou*.
Home Activity: Have your child give tell what each short *u* word means.

Name _____   **Multisyllabic Words**

The number of vowel sounds you hear in a word tells how many syllables are in the word.

sheep   chicken   kangaroo
1 syllable   2 syllables   3 syllables

Say each picture name. Write 1, 2, or 3 on the line to show how many syllables the word has.

1. 	_____	2. 	_____
3. 	_____	4. 	_____
5. 	_____	6. 	_____
7. 	_____	8. 	_____
9. 	_____	10. 	_____

Notes for Home: Your child identified the number of syllables in words.
Home Activity: Have your child say each word on this page aloud and clap to show the number of syllables in the word.

Name _____

**Review /ȯ/
Vowel Patterns *aw*, *ough***

> The letters *aw* and *ough* stand for the vowel sound in these words.
>
> th**aw**   **ough**t

Write the word that answers the question. Then circle the letters that stand for the vowel sound in the word.

1. Is a hawk or a fawn a baby deer? _____

2. Do you sip through a straw or thaw? _____

3. Do you draw or yawn when you are sleepy? _____

4. Do you cough or brought when you are sick? _____

5. Was the war bought or fought? _____

Notes for Home: Your child wrote words with the vowel patterns *aw* and *ough*.
Home Activity: Have your child identify the rhyming words on this page.

Review
Silent Letters: *gn, wh, wr*

Name _____

> In words like *design, whom,* and *wrap,* some letters are silent.

Write the word from the box that completes each sentence. Then underline the letter that is silent.

| sign | wrong | wrote | who | gnaw |

1. Rima _____ a letter to her cousin.

2. Did you see _____ won the race?

3. The _____ said "Two for One Sale!"

4. Dogs like to _____ on bones.

5. Something is _____ with the computer.

Notes for Home: Your child wrote words with silent letters. **Home Activity:** Have your child write a tongue twister using words with silent letters.

105

Name _____

**Schwa Sound
in *across* and *people***

The schwa sound can be spelled *a*.

across   **a**bout

The schwa sound can be spelled consonant + *le*.

peo**ple**   hum**ble**

Write the word with the schwa sound to complete each sentence.

1. Yuka lives in the apartment _____ me.
   below   above

2. Erica wore a _____ sweater.
   green   purple

3. Lions live in a _____ .
   jungle   zoo

4. Jorge ran _____ the track.
   around   on

5. The _____ soared in the sky.
   hawk   eagle

Notes for Home: Your child wrote words with the schwa sound spelled *a* and consonant + *le*.
Home Activity: Help your child think of other words with the schwa sound spelled *a* and consonant + *le*.

Name _____

Schwa Sound in *across* and *people*

The schwa sound in *across* is spelled *a*.
The schwa sound in *people* is spelled consonant + *le*.

Circle the word in each sentence that has the schwa sound spelled *a* or consonant + *le*. Write the word.

1. Put your toys away before bedtime. _____

2. The kettle was on the stove. _____

3. Pat likes to tell riddles. _____

4. It is about nine o'clock. _____

5. The stars seemed to twinkle. _____

Notes for Home: Your child wrote words with the schwa sound spelled *a* and consonant + *le*. **Home Activity:** Have your child underline the letter or letters that stand for the schwa sound in each word he or she wrote.

107

Name _____ Plural *-s* and *-es*

Add *-s* or *-es* to a word to show more than one.

Add *-s* to words like *house*.   house—hous**es**

Add *-es* to words that end in *s, ss, ch, sh,* or *x*.

   ax—ax**es**   church—church**es**
   bush—bush**es**   glass—glass**es**

Write the plural form of the picture name in the sentence.

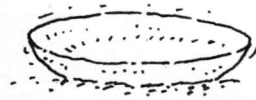 1. We washed many _____.

 2. The park has three _____.

 3. Two _____ slept in the den.

 4. The _____ are beautiful.

 5. Several _____ waited in line.

Notes for Home: Your child added *-s* and *-es* to make the plural forms of words.
Home Activity: Label two columns *-s* and *-es*. Take turns with your child writing a word and its plural form in each column.

Name _____   **Review Short *u*: *ou***

The letters *ou* stand for the short *u* vowel sound in words like *tough*.

The words below have the short *u* sound spelled *ou*. Find and circle each word in the puzzle.

| cousin | enough | southern | couple | trouble |
| touch | rough | country | young | double |

```
e w c o u n t r y r
n e o c o u p l e g
o s y o e t s w y o
u t h u t r a t k t
g h a s d o u b l e
h r s i y u r u m h
q o d n h b f b w n
a u f w n l t h a m
c g r a j e y e e u
t h i d o t o u c h
o b s o u t h e r n
y o u n g r g r e s
```

Notes for Home: Your child identified words with the short *u* sound spelled *ou*.
Home Activity: Have your child choose five words and write a sentence for each one.

Name _____   **Review Multisyllabic Words**

> Some words have one syllable: *cot, nurse.*
> Some words have two syllables: *summer, dentist.*
> Some words have three syllables: *umbrella, kangaroo.*

Write 1, 2, or 3 on the line to show how many syllables each word has. Then write the word with two syllables.

1. difficult   dime   dinner   _____
   _____   _____   _____

2. bottom   boot   bodyguard   _____
   _____   _____   _____

3. horn   hornet   horrible   _____
   _____   _____   _____

4. kimono   kitten   kite   _____
   _____   _____   _____

5. chain   character   camel   _____
   _____   _____   _____

Notes for Home: Your child identified words with one, two, or three syllables.
Home Activity: Have your child look through a magazine and cut out pictures whose names have one, two, or three syllables and sort them according to number of syllables.

Name _____   Vowel Digraph *ue*

> The letters *ue* stand for the vowel sound in *blue*.

Choose the word from the box that makes sense in the sentence and has the vowel sound in *blue*. Write the word.

| tissue | paste | guard | true | clues |
| hints | statue | handkerchief | glue | real |

1. Bring scissors and _____ to class.

   _____

2. Use the _____ to figure out the word's meaning.

   _____

3. A _____ stood outside of the building.

   _____

4. She wiped her nose with a _____.

   _____

5. The movie was based on a _____ story.

   _____

Notes for Home: Your child wrote words that have the vowel sound in *blue*.
Home Activity: Take turns with your child choosing a word from the box and making up a sentence for the word.

111

Name _____   **Vowel Digraph *ue***

> The letters *ue* spell the vowel sound in *blue*.

Follow the directions.

1. Write *blue*. Underline the letters that spell the vowel sound.

2. Change *b* to *g*. Write the new word. Underline the letters that spell the vowel sound.

3. Change *g* to *c*. Write the new word. Underline the letters that spell the vowel sound.

4. Change *cl* to *tr*. Write the new word. Underline the letters that spell the vowel sound.

5. Change *tr* to *s*. Write the new word. Underline the letters that spell the vowel sound.

Notes for Home: Your child wrote words that have the vowel sound in *blue*.
Home Activity: Have your child write a poem using two words from this page.

Name _____   **Schwa Sound in** *weather*

> The schwa sound can be spelled consonant + *er*.
>
> wea**ther**   fe**ver**

Underline the words that have the schwa sound spelled consonant + *er*. Then follow the directions.

across	hammer	seven	barrel	ladder
dinner	ahead	finger	cabin	water
kitchen	better	feather	beaver	jewel
diet	sweater	muffin	carrot	number

1. Write the word that names an animal that builds dams. _____

2. Write the word that names 1, 5, 8, 12, 37, or 124. _____

3. Write the word that names a tool for hitting. _____

4. Write the word that names a part of the hand. _____

5. Write the word that names a piece of clothing. _____

Notes for Home: Your child identified words that have the schwa sound spelled consonant + *er*. **Home Activity:** Together make a list of things around the house whose names have the schwa sound spelled consonant + *er*.

Name _____

Review Schwa Sound in *across* **and** *people*

> The schwa sound can be spelled *a* or consonant + *le*.
>
> **a**long   bri**dle**

Unscramble the letters to make a word that has the schwa sound spelled *a* or consonant + *le* and that matches the clue. Write the word.

1. not big — lleitt _____

2. from one side to the other — scasor _____

3. use it with thread — deenel _____

4. in front — aadhe _____

5. a color — lerpup _____

Notes for Home: Your child wrote words with the schwa sound spelled *a* or consonant − *le*. **Home Activity:** Have your child tell a story using the words *poodle, table, noodle, about,* and *alone.*

Name _____   Review Plural -s and -es

> Add -*s* or -*es* to a word to show more than one.
>
> nurse—nurse**s**   inch—inch**es**
> fox—fox**es**   bush—bush**es**   bus—bus**es**

Circle *s* or *es* to show how to make each picture name mean more than one.

1.  s   es
horse

2.  s   es
brush

3.  s   es
match

4.  s   es
rose

5.  s   es
peach

6.  s   es
purse

7.  s   es
box

8.  s   es
house

9.  s   es
dish

10.  s   es
glass

 **Notes for Home:** Your child identified -*s* and -*es* as the plural endings on words.
Home Activity: Have your child look through a magazine or newspaper, circle plural words, and list the words according to their -*s* and -*es* endings.

Name _____ Long *a: ei, eigh*

> The long *a* sound can be spelled *ei* as in *reindeer* or *eigh* as in *eight*.

Circle the word that has the same vowel sound as the picture name. Underline the letters that spell the vowel sound in the word.

1.		freight cap	2.	wrap weight
3.		veil vine	4.	reign pat
5.		sleigh try	6.	cannon neighbor
7.		vein march	8.	grand eighty
9.		beige stamp	10.	reindeer ham

Notes for Home: Your child identified words with the long *a* sound spelled *ei* and *eigh*.
Home Activity: Have your child choose four words from this page and make up a riddle for each one.

Name _____ Long *a: ei, eigh*

In the word *vein*, the letters *ei* spell the long *a* vowel sound.
In the word *eight*, the letters *eigh* spell the long *a* vowel sound.

Write the words to complete the puzzle.

reindeer   veil   beige   neighbor   eight

Across
2. seven plus one
3. person next door
4. light tan

Down
1. animal with antlers
5. worn over the face

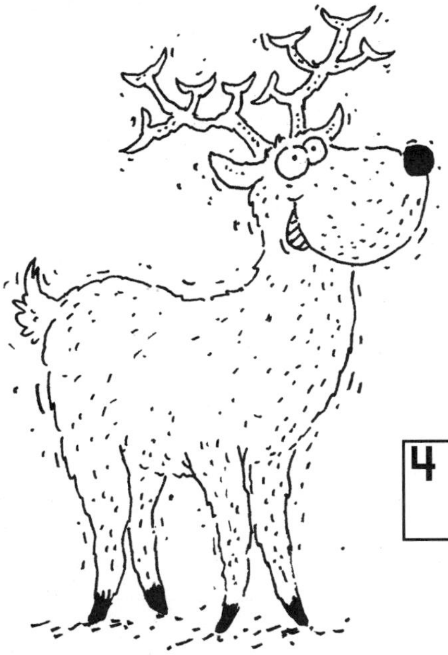

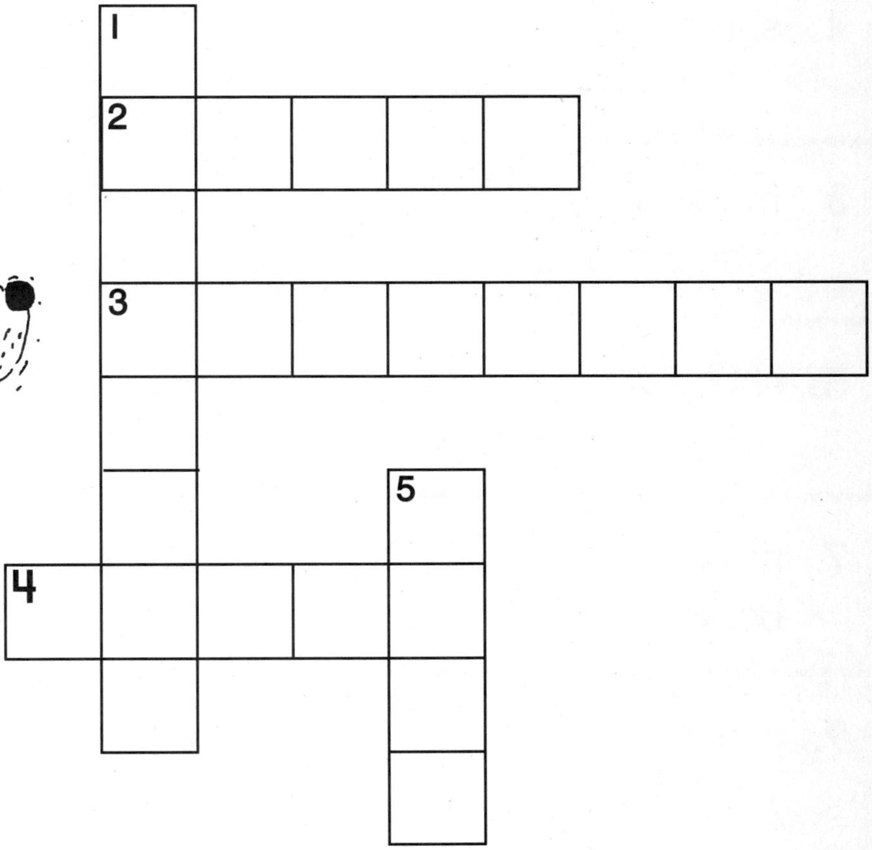

Notes for Home: Your child identified words with the long *a* sound spelled *ei* and *eigh*.
Home Activity: Have your child tell a story using the words *reindeer, eight, sleigh,* and *neighbor.*

Name _____

Words with Endings and Suffixes

Adding an ending or a suffix to a base word adds another syllable to the word.

high   one syllable   high + er = higher   two syllables
help   one syllable   help + less = helpless two syllables

Draw a line to divide each word between the base word and the ending or suffix. Then write the word that matches each clue.

| chooses | talking | smaller | sunless | darkest |
| restless | quickly | closes | pushes | helpful |

1. shuts _____

2. without sun _____

3. more than small _____

4. without rest _____

5. shoves _____

6. speaking _____

7. most dark _____

8. full of help _____

9. picks _____

10. with speed _____

Notes for Home: Your child identified words of more than one syllable that have suffixes and endings. **Home Activity:** Have your child look in a favorite book, find words that have the same endings or suffixes as the words on this page, and tell how many syllables each word has.

Name _____   **Review Vowel Digraph *ue***

The vowel sound in *blue* is spelled *ue*.

Circle the word that has the same vowel sound as the picture name. Then write the word and circle the letters that spell the vowel sound you hear in *blue*.

1.
   statue
   standing
   _____

2.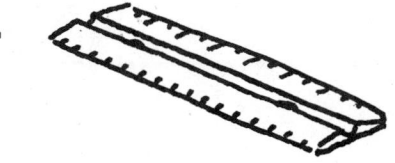
   cut
   clue
   _____

3.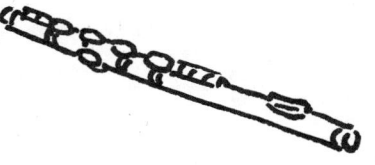
   true
   truck
   _____

4.
   taste
   tissue
   _____

5.
   glue
   glum
   _____

Notes for Home: Your child identified words that have the vowel sound in *blue*.
Home Activity: Have your child write a phrase using each circled word.

119

Name _____   **Review Schwa Sound in** *weather*

> The schwa sound can be spelled consonant + *er*.
>
> wat**er**   fea**ther**

Write the word that answers each clue. Then underline the letters that spell the schwa sound.

member   banner   chatter   order   tiger

1. talk quickly _____

2. a flag _____

3. a person belonging to a group _____

4. tell what to do _____

5. a large cat with stripes _____

Notes for Home: Your child identified words that have the schwa sound spelled consonant + *er*. **Home Activity:** Have your child make a banner using words with the schwa sound spelled consonant + *er*.

Name _____ Pattern *ex*

The letters *ex* spell the beginning sounds in these words.

explore   **ex**cite

Write a word from the box in place of the underlined word or words.

exit   next   explain   Texas   exact

1. Austin is the capital of <u>a large state</u>.    _____

2. The sign showed him the <u>way out</u>.    _____

3. My watch tells <u>correct</u> time.    _____

4. Her birthday is the <u>following</u> week.    _____

5. Can you <u>tell</u> how the machine works?    _____

Notes for Home: Your child wrote words with the *ex* pattern. **Home Activity:** Together with your child look through a magazine or newspaper for other words with the *ex* pattern. Make a list of the words you find.

121

Name _____   Pattern *ex*

> In words like *exercise* and *expert,* the letters *ex* stand for the beginning sounds.

Add *ex* to the letters to finish the word. Write the word.

1. the ind__ __ of the book

2. the state of T__ __as

3. n__ __t in line

4. __ __it from the room

5. an __ __act copy

6. an __ __tra pair of socks

7. a good __ __ample

8. an __ __pert in math

9. everyone __ __cept me

10. __ __plore the cave

Notes for Home: Your child completed words with the *ex* pattern. **Home Activity:** Challenge your child to tell a story using the words *explain, excellent, extra, example,* and *experiment.*

Name _____ **Prefixes** *un-, dis-, re-*

> A prefix is a word part added to the beginning of a word. Adding a prefix like *un-*, *dis-*, or *re-* changes the meaning of the word.
>
> un + happy = **un**happy   not happy, the opposite of *happy*
> dis + loyal = **dis**loyal   not loyal, the opposite of *loyal*
> re + wind = **re**wind   to wind again

Add the prefix to the underlined word. Write the new word.

1. **(dis)** to not like   _____

2. **(dis)** the opposite of obey   _____

3. **(re)** to fill again   _____

4. **(un)** the opposite of safe   _____

5. **(un)** not lucky   _____

Notes for Home: Your child wrote words with the prefixes *un-*, *dis-*, and *re-*.
Home Activity: Have your child choose a word from the page and draw a picture to show how the meaning changed when the prefix *un-*, *dis-*, or *re-* was added.

Name _____   **Review Long *a*: *ei*, *eigh***

> The letters *ei* and *eigh* spell the long *a* sound in *rein* and *sleigh*.

Unscramble the letters to make a word from the list that has the long *a* sound spelled *ei* or *eigh*. Write the word.

    eight   freight   veil   beige   weight

1. The bride wore a lace *leiv*. _____

2. He washed his *geeib* shirt. _____

3. The bowl held *tigeh* eggs. _____

4. The *rifthge* train hauled coal. _____

5. What is the *gwieth* of that box? _____

Notes for Home: Your child identified words with the long *a* sound spelled *ei* and *eigh*.
Home Activity: Have your child rewrite each sentence on this page as a question and underline the long *a* words.

Name _____

Words with Endings and Suffixes

> Adding an ending or a suffix to a base word usually adds another syllable to the word.
>
> | | |
> |---|---|
> | match | one syllable |
> | match + es = matches | two syllables |
> | cold | one syllable |
> | cold + er = colder | two syllables |

Follow the signs to make a new word. Write the word. Then in the box write the number of syllables you hear.

1. finish + es _____ ☐

2. run + ing _____ ☐

3. swift + ly _____ ☐

4. beauty + ful _____ ☐

5. hopped − ed + ing _____ ☐

Notes for Home: Your child identified words of more than one syllable that have suffixes and endings. **Home Activity:** Have your child add an ending or suffix to *forget, wish,* and *sudden* and tell how many syllables each new word has.

Name _____ Long *e: ie, ey*

> The long *e* vowel sound in *niece* is spelled *ie*.
> The long *e* vowel sound in *valley* is spelled *ey*.

Draw a line to match each picture with its name. Circle the letters that stand for the long *e* sound in each word.

1.    field

2.    donkey

3.    cookie

4. 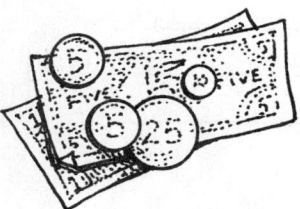   money

5.    monkey

Notes for Home: Your child identified words that have the long *e* vowel sound spelled *ie* and *ey*. **Home Activity:** Have your child choose two words from this page and make up a riddle for each one.

Name _____   Long *e: ie, ey*

In the word *grief,* the letters *ie* spell the long *e* vowel sound.
In the word *trolley,* the letters *ey* spell the long *e* vowel sound.

Underline the words that have the long *e* sound spelled *ie* or *ey*. Then follow the directions.

alley	shy	chief	field	team
brief	pulley	niece	they	piece
money	obey	beige	key	hockey

1. Write the word that rhymes with *shield*. _____

2. Write the word that names a relative. _____

3. Write the word that names something that opens a lock. _____

4. Write the word that names a game played on ice. _____

5. Write the word that means a part of something. _____

Notes for Home: Your child identified words that have the long *e* vowel sound spelled *ie* and *ey*. **Home Activity:** Challenge your child to think of clues for the five underlined words that were not written on the page.

127

Name _____   **Consonants *gh, ph, lf/f/***

> The *f* sound can be spelled *gh*, *ph*, and *lf*.
>
>   cou**gh**   go**ph**er   ha**lf**way

Write the word that answers the question. Circle the letters that stand for the *f* sound.

1. Does sandpaper feel rough or enough? _____

2. Have you had enough or tough when you are full? _____

3. Does a dolphin or an elephant live in the ocean? _____

4. Do you use a phone or a graph to call a friend? _____

5. Is a calf or a nephew a baby cow? _____

Notes for Home: Your child identified words that have the *f* sound spelled *gh*, *ph*, and *lf*.
Home Activity: Have your child write sentences using the words *tough*, *alphabet*, and *golf*.

Name _____   Review Pattern *ex*

The letters *ex* can be at the beginning, in the middle, or at the end of words.

Find and circle the *ex* words in the puzzle. Then write the *ex* word that goes with each meaning clue.

examine
extra
index
explode
next

b	t	r	o	l	m	e
e	a	x	i	e	d	x
x	i	k	e	x	y	p
s	n	e	x	t	j	l
y	d	q	d	r	u	o
t	e	g	h	a	x	d
e	x	a	m	i	n	e

1. following
   _____

   _____

2. part of a book
   _____

   _____

3. look at carefully
   _____

   _____

4. to burst
   _____

   _____

5. more than enough
   _____

   _____

Notes for Home: Your child wrote words with the *ex* pattern. **Home Activity:** Have your child write a question using each of the *ex* words on this page.

Name _____   **Prefixes -un, -dis, -re**

> The prefixes *un-* and *dis-* mean *not* or *opposite of*.
> The prefix *re-* means *to do again*.
>
> the opposite of *like*   **un**like
> not respectful   **dis**respectful
> to play again   **re**play

Add the prefix to the base word to form a new word. Use the new words to complete the sentences.

(un) wrap   **(dis)** honest   **(re)** load
(un) ripe   **(re)** heat

1. The _____ person stole the money.

2. Can you _____ the soup?

3. Is that green banana _____ ?

4. Jeff wants to _____ his present.

5. The driver will _____ the truck.

Notes for Home: Your child wrote words with the prefixes *un-*, *dis-*, and *re-*.
Home Activity: Have your child add *un-*, *dis-*, or *re-* to these words: *kind, agree, build*.

130

Name _____   Long *e: ei*

In the word *receipt*, the letters *ei* spell the long *e* vowel sound.

Add *ei* to the letters to finish the word. Write the word.

1. Flying kites is Mike's l__ __sure activity.  _____

2. You get prot__ __n from meat.  _____

3. She painted the c__ __ling.  _____

4. Did you rec__ __ve a gift?  _____

5. The player s__ __zed the ball.  _____

Notes for Home: Your child wrote words with the long *e* sound spelled *ei*.
Home Activity: Take turns with your child choosing a word from the page and using it in a sentence.

Name _____   **Long e: ei**

> The long *e* vowel sound can be spelled *ei* as in *protein*.

Follow the directions. Use the words from the box. Then circle the letters that stand for the long *e* sound.

| ceiling | seize | receipt | leisure | receive |

1. Write the word that names time you spend not working. _____

2. Write the word that means "get." _____

3. Write the word that names part of a room. _____

4. Write the word that means "grab." _____

5. Write the word that names the paper you get when you buy something. _____

Notes for Home: Your child identified words with the long *e* sound spelled *ei*.
Home Activity: Scramble the letters of each word in the box and have your child unscramble and write the words.

Name _____   Plural -*es*

For some words that end in *f* or *fe,* the *f* or *fe* is changed to *v,* and *-es* is added to show more than one.

> half—hal**ves**

Write the word that names the picture. Then add *-es* to make the word mean more than one. Write the new word.

1. I raked the 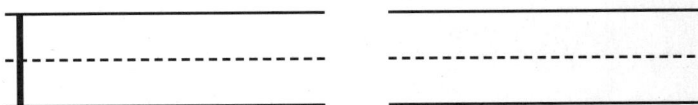 into a big pile.

   l_____   _____

2. She put tw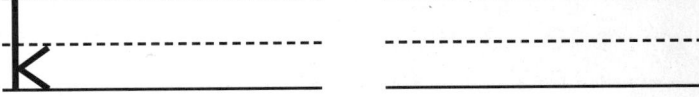 on the table.

   k_____   _____

3. Seth baked three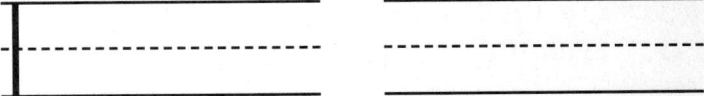

   l_____   _____

4. The 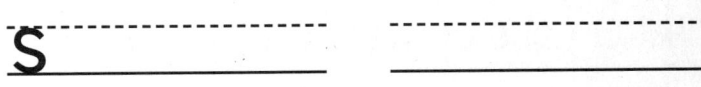 were ready.

   s_____   _____

5. The  are sleeping.

   w_____   _____

Notes for Home: Your child added *-es* to make the plural forms of words ending in *f* or *fe*.
Home Activity: Have your child form the plurals of *elf, calf,* and *scarf* and write a sentence using each word.

133

Name _____   Review Long *e: ie, ey*

> The long *e* sound can be spelled *ie* and *ey*.
> ni**e**ce   mon**ey**

Write the word that completes each sentence and has the long *e* sound spelled *ie* or *ey*.

1. My dad is a police _____.
   chief   officer

2. The bees made _____.
   noise   honey

3. The farmer planted a _____ of corn.
   field   row

4. Smoke came out of the _____.
   chimney   roof

5. His speech was _____.
   long   brief

Notes for Home: Your child identified words that have the long *e* vowel sound spelled *ie* and *ey*. **Home Activity:** Write the headings *ie* and *ey* on paper and help your child think of words to write under each heading.

134

Name _____   Review Consonants *gh, ph, lf* /f/

> The *f* sound can be spelled *gh*, *ph*, and *lf*.
>
> rou**gh**   gra**ph**   go**lf**

Use the words in the box to complete the puzzle.

| half | laugh | enough | gopher | autograph |

Across
4. signing your name
5. one of two parts

Down
1. an animal that lives in the ground
2. just the right amount
3. what a joke makes you do

Notes for Home: Your child identified words that have the *f* sound spelled *gh, ph,* or *lf*.
Home Activity: Help your child make a list of other words that have the *f* sound spelled *gh, ph,* or *lf*.

135

Name _____   r-Controlled Vowels: *air, are*

> The letters *air* and *are* stand for the vowel sound in these words.
>
> f**air**   sp**are**

Write the word that names each picture. Circle the letters that stand for the vowel sound.

pair   chair   hair   mare   square

1. [square picture]   _____   air   are

2. [chair picture]   _____   air   are

3. [hair picture]   _____   air   are

4. [mare picture]   _____   air   are

5. [socks picture]   _____   air   are

Notes for Home: Your child identified words with the *air* and *are* vowel patterns.
Home Activity: Have your child write a poem using rhyming *air* and *are* words.

Name _____   r-Controlled Vowels: *air, are*

> In words like *hair* and *dare,* the letters *air* and *are* stand for the vowel sound.

Write the word that matches the meaning and has the vowel sound in *hair*. Circle the letters that spell the vowel sound.

1. to look at something   gaze / stare   _____

2. something to sit on   chair / couch   _____

3. to fix something   repair / mend   _____

4. to make a loud sound   shout / blare   _____

5. two that go together   pair / couple   _____

Notes for Home: Your child identified words with the *air* and *are* vowel patterns.
Home Activity: Have your child make a list of words that rhyme with *care*.

Name _____   Consonants: *dge* /j/

> The letters *dge* spell the *j* sound in *hedge*.

Write the word from the box that completes each sentence. Underline the letters that spell the ending *j* sound.

| bridge | judge | fudge | ledge | badge |

1. The police officer wore a shiny _____ .

2. A new _____ was built over the river.

3. Sara put nuts in the _____ .

4. I set the plant on the window _____ .

5. The _____ spoke to the jury.

Notes for Home: Your child wrote words in which /j/ is spelled *dge*. **Home Activity:** Have your child write a tongue twister using the words *badge, budge,* and *bridge.*

Name _____   Review Long *e: ei*

> The letters *ei* spell the long *e* sound in *receipt*.

Find five words in the puzzle with the long *e* sound spelled *ei*.
Circle each word in the puzzle. Then write the word.

```
r  i  e  h  t  r  e
e  r  o  n  y  t  u
c  e  i  l  i  n  g
e  c  w  e  r  o  k
i  e  w  i  r  a  c
v  i  l  s  k  e  k
e  p  f  u  a  m  t
i  t  h  r  r  u  u
d  e  c  e  i  v  e
```

1. _____

2. _____

3. _____

4. _____

5. _____

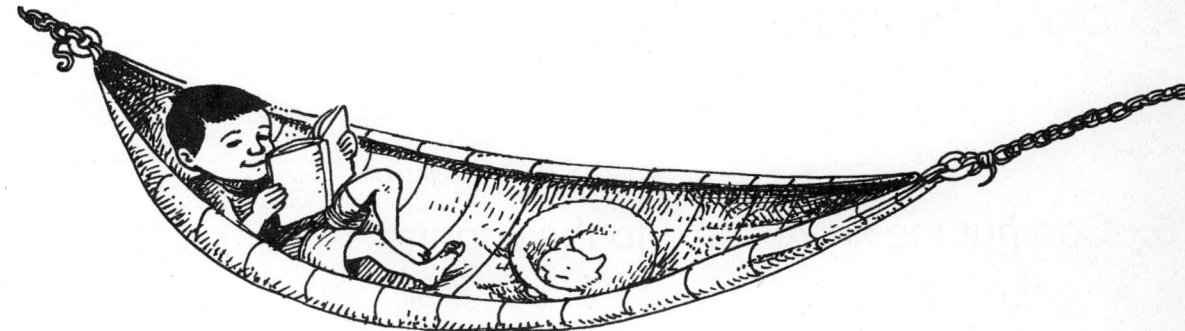

Notes for Home: Your child identified words that have the long *e* vowel sound spelled *ei*.
Home Activity: Give a clue for each of the circled words and have your child name the *ei* word that goes with the clue.

Name _____   Review Plural -es

> To form the plural of some words ending in *f* or *fe*, *f* or *fe* is changed to *v*, and *-es* is added.
>
> wi**fe**—wi**ves**

Write the plural form of the underlined word.

1. The <u>loaf</u> of bread was freshly baked.   _____

2. The <u>wolf</u> howled at the moon.   _____

3. The dictionary is on that <u>shelf</u>.   _____

Write the singular form of the underlined word.

4. Did the tree's <u>leaves</u> turn red?   _____

5. Carl put the <u>knives</u> next to the spoons.   _____

Notes for Home: Your child wrote the plural and singular forms of words ending in *f* and *fe*.
Home Activity: Encourage your child to write a short story using as many plural words as possible from this page.

Name _____

Long Vowels at the Ends of Syllables

> A vowel at the end of a syllable in a word stands for a long vowel sound.
>
>   **a**/ble   di/et   b**o**/nus
>   long *a*   long *i*   long *o*

Circle the long vowel sound you hear at the end of a syllable in each word.

1. real
   long *a*   long *e*   long *u*

2. dial
   long *a*   long *e*   long *i*

3. cradle
   long *a*   long *e*   long *o*

4. poet
   long *a*   long *e*   long *o*

5. uniform
   long *i*   long *o*   long *u*

6. cereal
   long *a*   long *e*   long *o*

7. bacon
   long *a*   long *o*   long *u*

8. program
   long *a*   long *e*   long *o*

9. title
   long *e*   long *i*   long *o*

10. music
    long *a*   long *i*   long *u*

Notes for Home: Your child identified long vowel sounds at the ends of syllables in words.
Home Activity: Ask your child to name the long vowel sound in each of these words: *paper, broken, tiger, unit.*

Long Vowels at the Ends of Syllables

Name _____

> Vowels at the ends of syllables stand for long vowel sounds.
>
> ba/con   e/ven   pi/lot
> long *a* long *e* long *i*

Write the name of each picture. Circle the letter that stands for a long vowel sound.

| paper | uniform | table | music | pliers |
| lion | cereal | zero | banjo | cradle |

1. banjo
2. cereal
3. table
4. music
5. pliers
6. paper
7. uniform
8. zero
9. cradle
10. lion

Notes for Home: Your child wrote words with long vowel sounds at the ends of syllables.
Home Activity: Together with your child write other words like those on the page. Check them in a dictionary.

Name _____   **Consonants** *ch* /k/, *sch* /sk/

> The letters *ch* spell /k/ in *chord*.
> The letters *sch* spell /sk/ in *schedule*.

Underline the words that have /k/ spelled *ch* as in *chord* or /sk/ spelled *sch* as in *schedule*. Then write the underlined words in the correct list.

chalk	risk	chemist
school	shadow	track
fresh	scheme	score
scream	color	stomach
chorus	sketch	bench

/k/ spelled *ch*   **/sk/ spelled *sch***

1. _____ 4. _____

2. _____ 5. _____

3. _____

Notes for Home: Your child identified words in which /k/ is spelled *ch* and /sk/ is spelled *sch*.
Home Activity: Have your child use each word he or she wrote in a sentence.

Name _____   r-Controlled Vowels: *air, are*

> The letters *air* and *are* stand for the vowel sound in *stairs* and *hare*.

Write a word from the list to complete each sentence. Then circle the letters that stand for the vowel sound.

spare   rare   repair   share   pair

1. Will you ____ your fruit with me?

2. I bought a new ____ of shoes.

3. Can you ____ the broken radio?

4. He put the ____ tire on the car.

5. Tara collects ____ stamps.

Notes for Home: Your child wrote words with the *air* and *are* vowel patterns.
Home Activity: Have your child write a newspaper headline using words from this page.

Name _____   **Review Consonants *dge* /j/**

> The letters *dge* stand for the *j* sound in *budge*.

Write the word that answers the clue and has the *j* sound spelled *dge*.

bridge	jury	badge	toffee	uniform
fence	fudge	current	judge	hedge

1. A garden may have this. _____

2. A court of law has this. _____

3. A police officer has this. _____

4. A candy shop has this. _____

5. A river may have this. _____

Notes for Home: Your child identified words in which the *j* sound is spelled *dge*.
Home Activity: Have your child write clues for these *dge* words: *ledge, ridge, budge*.

Name _____

r-Controlled Vowels: *ear* /ėr/ and *our* /our/

> The letters *ear* stand for the vowel sound in *earn*.
> The letters *our* stand for the vowel sound in *flour*.

Write the word from the box that belongs in each group and has the vowel sound in *earn* or *flour*.

Pluto	day	learn	hunt	hour
sour	search	hot	Earth	know

1. study, practice, _____

2. salty, sweet, _____

3. Mars, Venus, _____

4. minute, second, _____

5. seek, look for, _____

Notes for Home: Your child wrote words with the *ear* and *our* vowel patterns.
Home Activity: Have your child circle the letters that stand for the vowel sound in each word he or she wrote on the page.

Name _____

r-Controlled Vowels: *ear* /ėr/ and *our* /our/

In *earn*, the letters *ear* stand for the vowel sound.
In *flour*, the letters *our* stand for the vowel sound.

Circle the words that have the same vowel sound and pattern as *earn* or *flour*. Then write the circled words to complete the sentences.

| court | hour | pearl | round | term |
| near | heard | fort | learn | sour |

1. We _____ a dog barking.

2. Omar came home an _____ late.

3. The ring has a _____ on it.

4. The baby will _____ to walk.

5. A lemon tastes very _____ .

Notes for Home: Your child wrote words with the *ear* and *our* vowel patterns.
Home Activity: Have your child make up two rhymes using the word pairs *earn/learn* and *sour/our*.

147

Name _____ Syllable Pattern *tion*

The letters *tion* make a syllable in words.

| petition | dictionary | evaluation |
| pe/ti/**tion** | dic/**tion**/ar/y | e/val/u/a/**tion** |

Add the letters *tion* to make another syllable in each word. Write the whole word.

1. ac/_____

2. col/lec/_____

3. so/lu/_____

4. frac/_____

5. di/rec/_____

6. cau/_____

7. na/_____/al

8. pro/tec/_____

9. po/si/_____

10. e/mo/_____/al

Notes for Home: Your child wrote words that have *tion* as a syllable.
Home Activity: Take turns with your child naming *tion* words like those on the page.

Name _____

Review Long Vowels at the Ends of Syllables

If a vowel is at the end of a syllable in a word, it can stand for a long vowel sound.

| ve/to | long e | long o |
| tor/na/do | long a | long o |

Write the word that completes each sentence. Circle each letter that stands for a long vowel sound. *Hint:* Each word has more than one long vowel sound.

stereo   idea   radio   piano   video

1. A local _____ station is having a talent contest.

2. I could win a _____ with speakers.

3. I could win a _____ camera.

4. But I have no _____ what I can do.

5. I know! I'll play a song on the _____ .

Notes for Home: Your child wrote words with long vowel sounds at the ends of syllables.
Home Activity: Have your child write a sentence using at least two of the long vowel words on the page.

149

Name _____

Review Consonants
ch /k/, *sch* /sk/

The letters *ch* can spell /k/ as in *chemist*.
The letters *sch* can spell /sk/ as in *scheme*.

Write the words to complete the paragraph. Circle the letters that spell /k/ as in *chemist* or /sk/ as in *scheme*.

chord   schedule   school   stomach   chorus

I have a busy (1.) _____ on Tuesdays.

From 8 until 3:30, I am at (2.) _____. Then I sing

in a (3.) _____. This Tuesday I was so busy I

missed lunch. At practice, when Mrs. Nuñez played a

(4.) _____ on the piano, my (5.) _____

growled really loud—right on cue! Everyone laughed.

Notes for Home: Your child wrote words in which *ch* spelled /k/ or *sch* spelled /sk/.
Home Activity: Together with your child make up a funny story using the *ch* and *sch* words on the page.

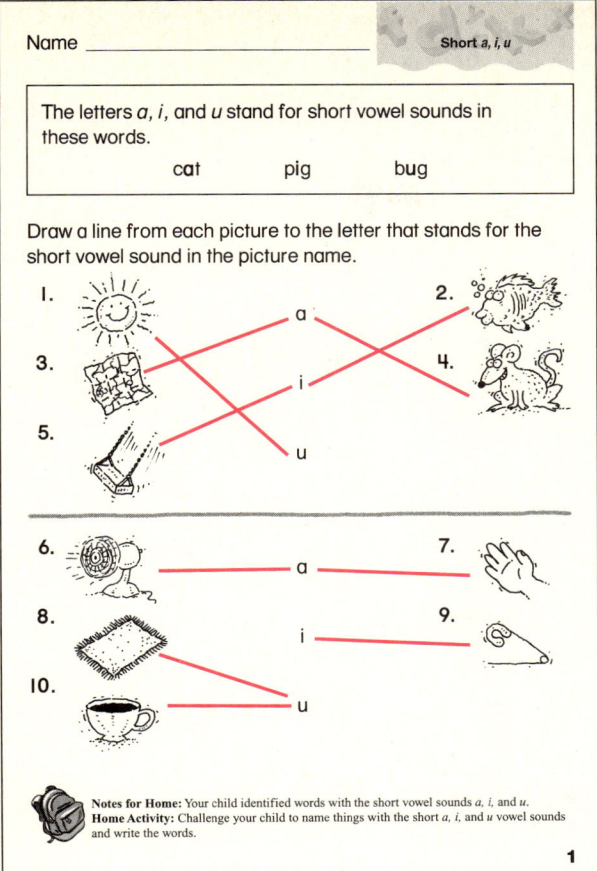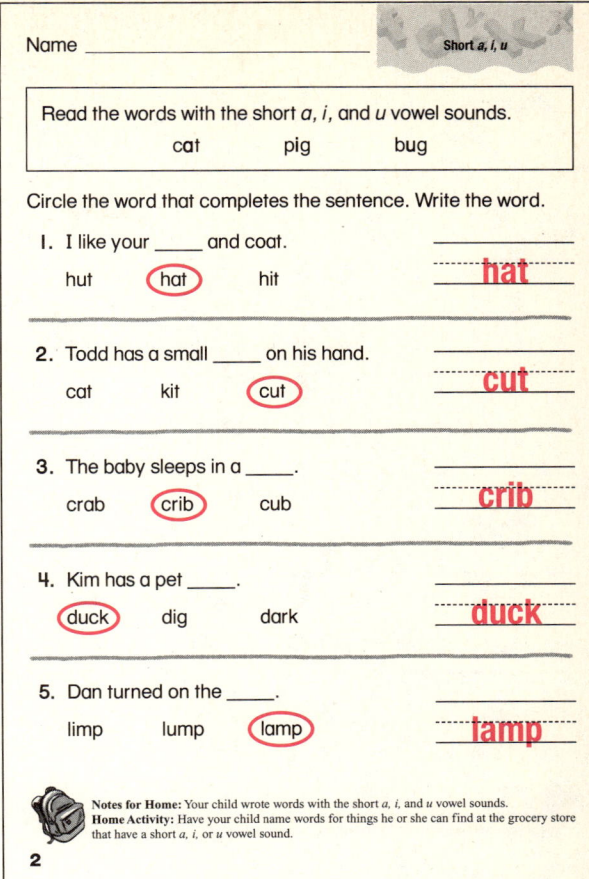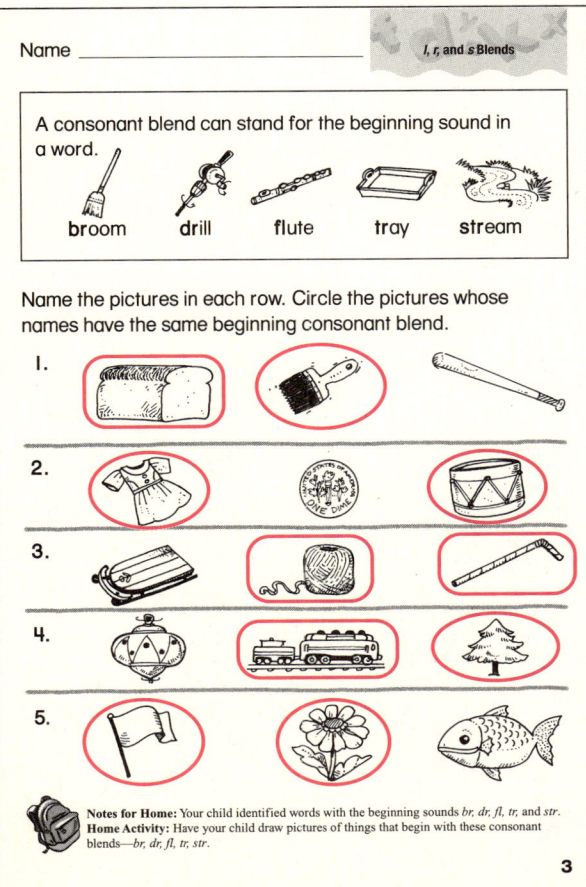

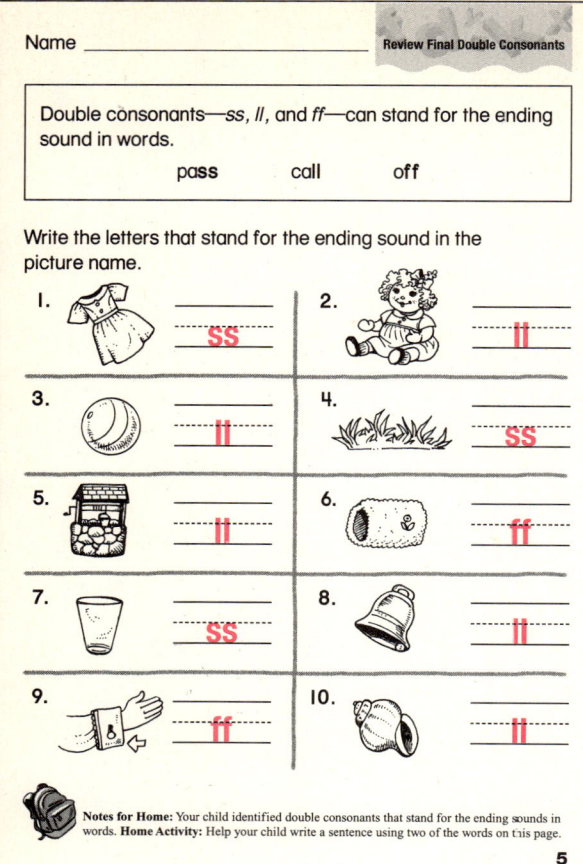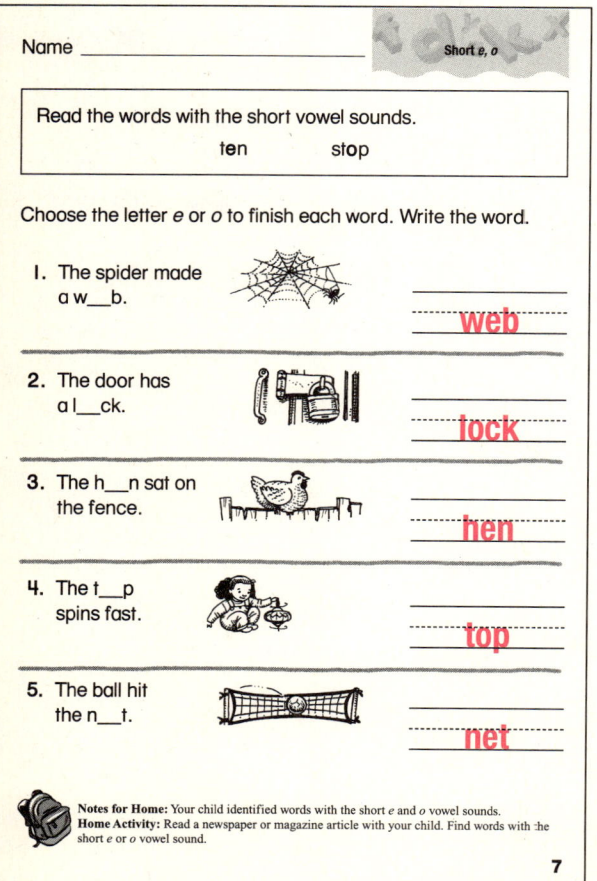

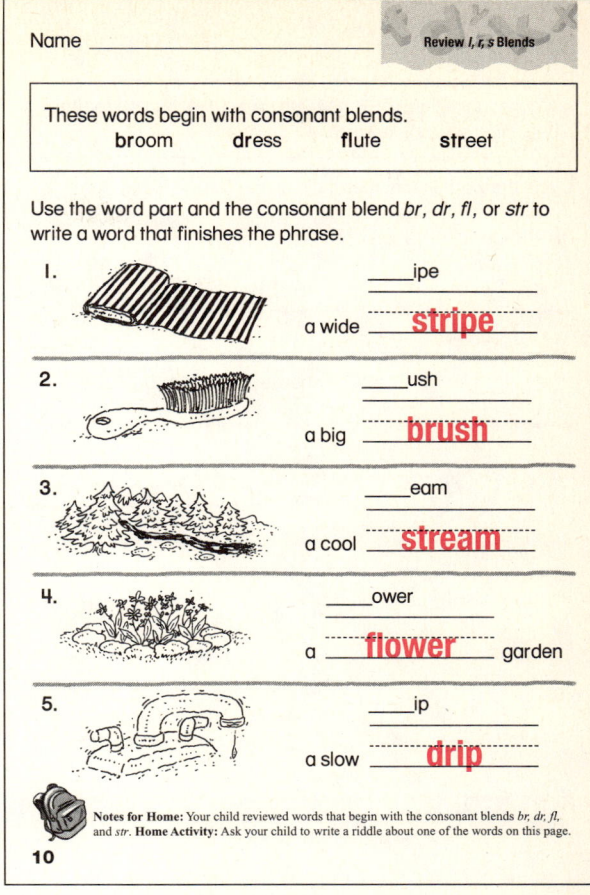

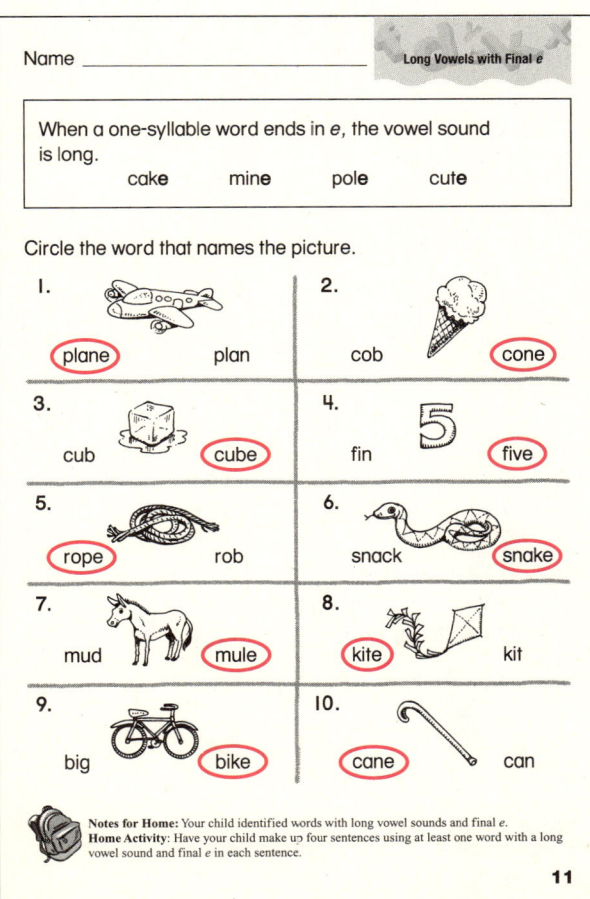

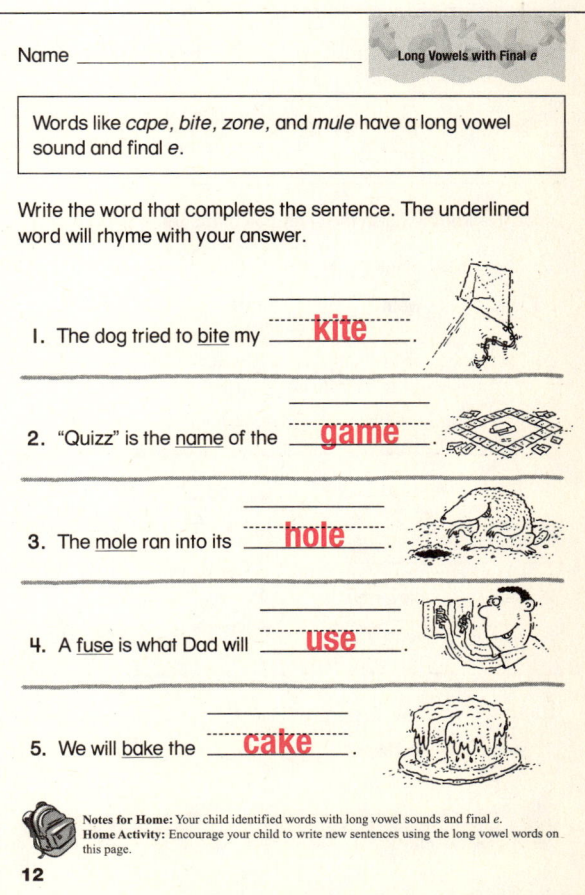

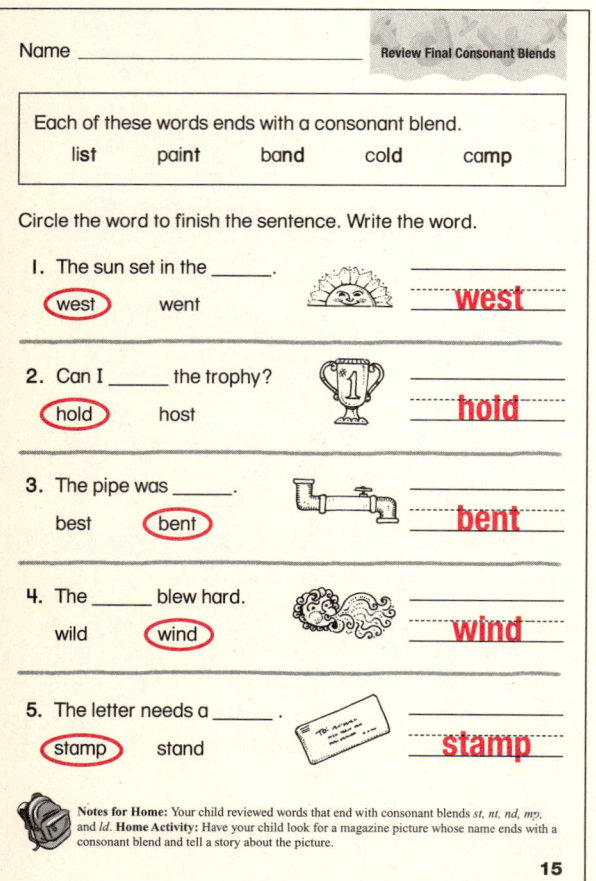
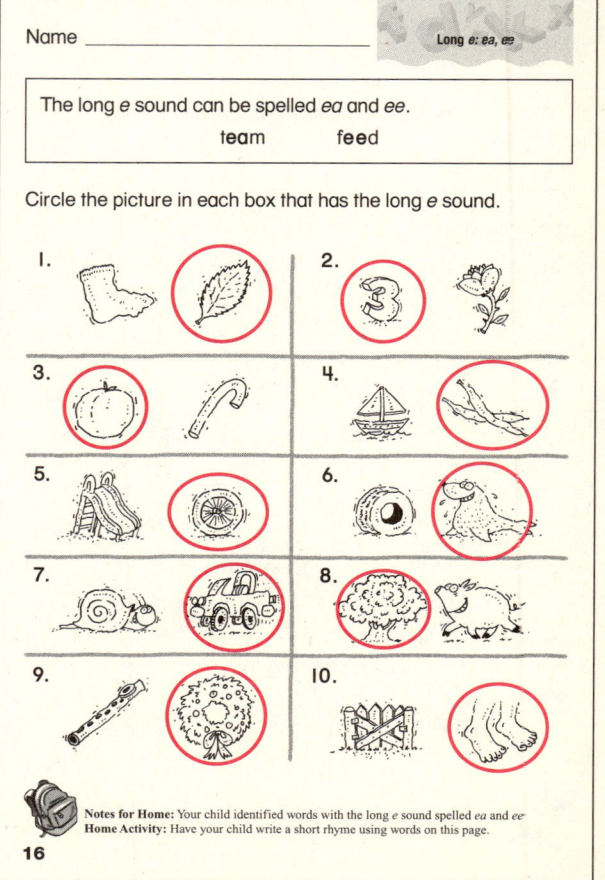

154 Answers

Page 17 — Long e: ea, ee

The long e sound can be spelled *ea* and *ee*.
bea**ch**   **thr**ee

Look at each picture. Choose a word from the box to complete the sentence. Write the word.

beans   green   weed   cream   peach

1. Who will pick a **peach** ?
2. Lin pulled up a **weed** .
3. The ice **cream** is melting.
4. The grass is **green** .
5. The **beans** are good to eat.

Page 18 — Final Consonant Digraphs

A consonant digraph—*ch*, *ng*, *nk*, *sh*, and *th*—can stand for the ending sound in a word.

Look at the letters. Circle the picture whose name ends with that sound.

1. ch — (peach circled)
2. ng — (swing circled)
3. nk — (pig/bank circled)
4. sh — (brush circled)
5. th — (moth circled)

Page 19 — Review Long Vowels with Final e

Words that end in *e* usually have a long vowel sound.
mate   ride   mule   hose

Circle the word that completes each sentence.

1. I can't find the roll of _____.   tap   (tape)
2. Ted went down the _____ in the park.   sled   (slide)
3. The bear slept in the _____.   cab   (cave)
4. The little cub was _____.   cut   (cute)
5. There is a _____ in your sweater.   (hole)   hill
6. An elephant is a _____ animal.   hug   (huge)
7. Do you _____ to ride your bike?   (like)   lake
8. The _____ swam in the ocean.   (whale)   while
9. Put the pan on the _____.   stop   (stove)
10. You use your _____ to smell things.   not   (nose)

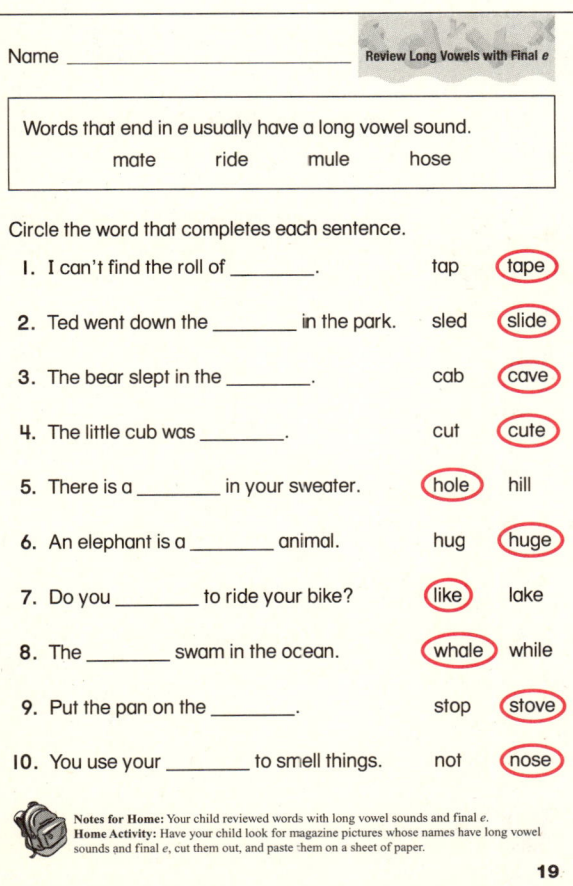

Page 20 — Review Initial Consonant Digraphs

Say each word and listen to the beginning sound.
chair   **th**umb   **sh**oe   **wh**ale

Write the word that goes with each clue.

cheer   thunder   sheep   whisper   chicken

1. a quiet sound only one person can hear — **whisper**
2. makes a noise that sounds like "b-a-a" — **sheep**
3. a rumbling sound during a storm — **thunder**
4. the sound at a game when your team wins — **cheer**
5. makes a cluck, cluck sound — **chicken**

Answers 155

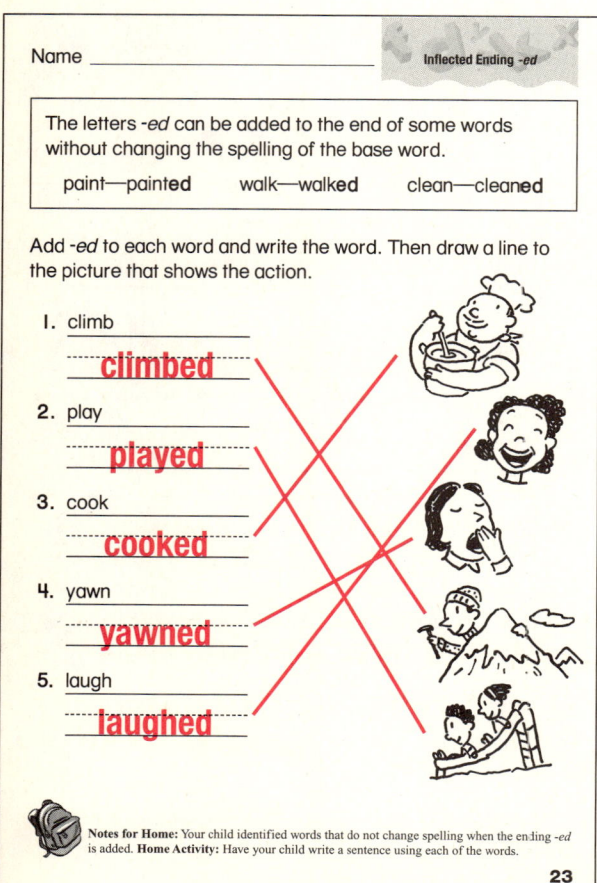
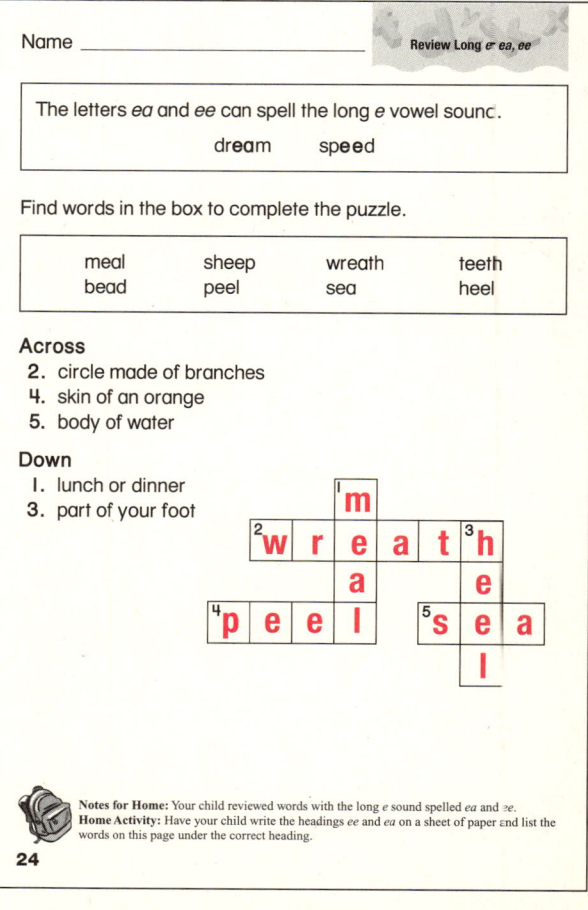

Review Final Consonant Digraphs

The letters *ch*, *ng*, *sh*, and *th* stand for the ending sounds in these words.

lun**ch** ri**ng** pu**sh** boo**th**

Find five words in the puzzle that end with *ch*, *ng*, *sh*, or *th*. Circle each word in the puzzle. Then write the word.

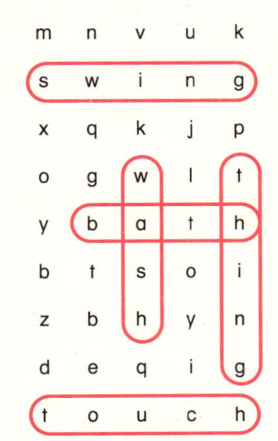

1. swing
2. bath
3. wash
4. thing
5. touch

Order of answers may vary.

 Notes for Home: Your child reviewed consonant digraphs that stand for ending sounds in words. **Home Activity:** Have your child write words that end in *ch*, *ng*, *sh*, or *th* and then draw a picture to show the meaning of the words.

25

Long *a*: *a, ai, ay*

The letters *a*, *ai*, and *ay* can spell the long *a* vowel sound.

t**a**ble p**ai**l st**ay**

Circle the word that names each picture and has the long *a* sound.

1.	snow / **snail**	2.	**paint** / pint
3.	he / **hay**	4.	pan / **paper**
5.	ran / **ray**	6.	**day** / dime
7.	track / **train**	8.	bag / **baby**
9.	**tray** / trap	10.	**sail** / seal

 **Notes for Home:** Your child identified words that have the long *a* sound spelled *a*, *ai*, or *ay*. **Home Activity:** Encourage your child to choose five words from this page and use each one in a sentence.

26

Long *a*: *a, ai, ay*

Words like *paper*, *mail*, and *day* have the long *a* sound spelled *a*, *ai*, and *ay*.

Find a word in the box that rhymes with the underlined word in each sentence. Write the word. Then say the whole rhyme.

stain today table clay pail

1. The cat put its <u>tail</u> in a red ____**pail**____.
2. This is the <u>way</u> to mold your ____**clay**____.
3. It's wet and <u>gray</u> outside ____**today**____.
4. The <u>rain</u> made a big wet ____**stain**____.
5. The <u>cable</u> is behind the ____**table**____.

 Notes for Home: Your child identified words that have the long *a* sound spelled *a*, *ai*, or *ay*. **Home Activity:** Have your child write *table*, *rain*, and *way* across the top of a sheet of paper and then find and write words with long *a* sound spelled the same as each word.

27

Inflected Endings -*es*, -*ing*, and -*s*

The letters -*es*, -*ing*, and -*s* can be added to the end of some words without changing the spelling of the base word.

hatch—hatch**es** fall—fall**ing** sit—sit**s**

Add the ending to the new word. Write the new word to finish the phrase.

1. tie   ____**ties**____ her shoe (-*s*)
2. search ____**searching**____ for a lost dog (-*ing*)
3. walk   ____**walks**____ to school (-*s*)
4. knock ____**knocking**____ on a door (-*ing*)
5. scratch ____**scratches**____ an itch (-*es*)

Notes for Home: Your child wrote words that do not change spelling when the ending -*es*, -*ing*, or -*s* is added. **Home Activity:** Have your child think of words that rhyme with the words from this page and then form new words by adding -*es*, -*ing*, or -*s*.

28

Answers **157**

Page 29 — Review Long e: e, y

The long *e* sound can be spelled *e* or *y*.
be   hungry

Read the riddles. Write answers that have long *e*.

open	country	little	we	him
tiny	empty	he	farm	us

1. Where do horses and cows live? **country**
2. What size is a mouse? **tiny**
3. What is a box if it has nothing in it? **empty**
4. What is a word for a friend and me? **we**
5. What is a word for a boy? **he**

Page 30 — Review Inflected Ending -ed

Words like *jump* and *scold* do not change their spelling when *-ed* is added.
jump—jump**ed**   scold—scold**ed**

Underline the word that will correctly complete the sentence when *-ed* is added. Then write the word with *-ed*.

1. Aunt Erica ___ the car.
   sail   <u>wax</u>   **waxed**
2. We ___ Dad in the yard.
   <u>help</u>   hop   **helped**
3. Troy ___ the picture.
   climb   <u>paint</u>   **painted**
4. The dog ___ loudly.
   <u>bark</u>   talk   **barked**
5. My sisters ___ the garage.
   jump   <u>clean</u>   **cleaned**

Page 31 — Long i: i, igh, y, ie

The long *i* sound can spelled *i*, *igh*, *y*, or *ie*.
iris   light   fry   pie

In each row, circle the picture that goes with the word. Then say the word.

1. light
2. night
3. fly
4. tie
5. high

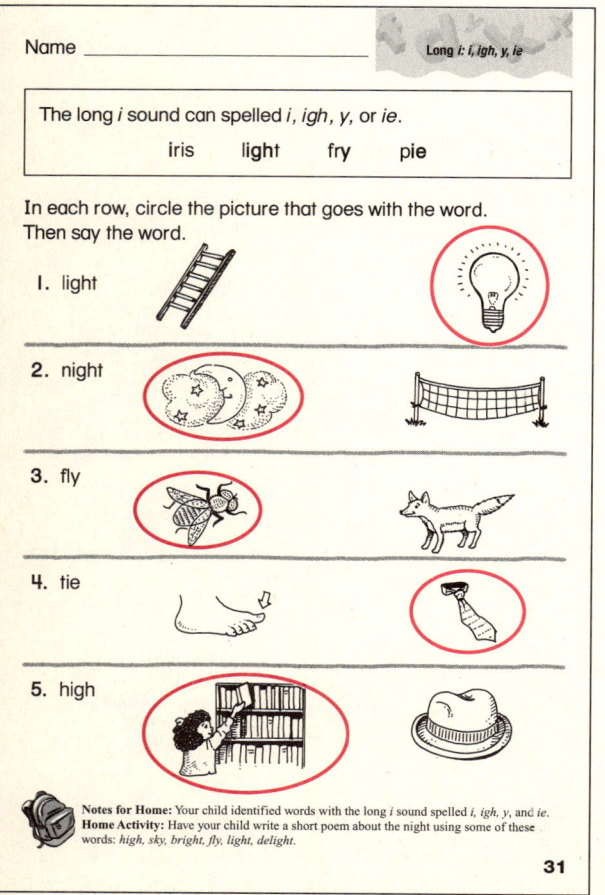

Page 32 — Long i: i, igh, y, ie

The letters *i*, *igh*, *y*, and *ie* can spell the long *i* sound.
mind   high   cry   tie

Write each word from the box under the word with the same vowel pattern.

| right | find | why | pie | idea |

List 1 — Words like *mind*
1. **idea**
2. **find**

List 2 — Words like *high*
3. **right**

List 3 — Words like *cry*
4. **why**

List 4 — Words like *tie*
5. **pie**

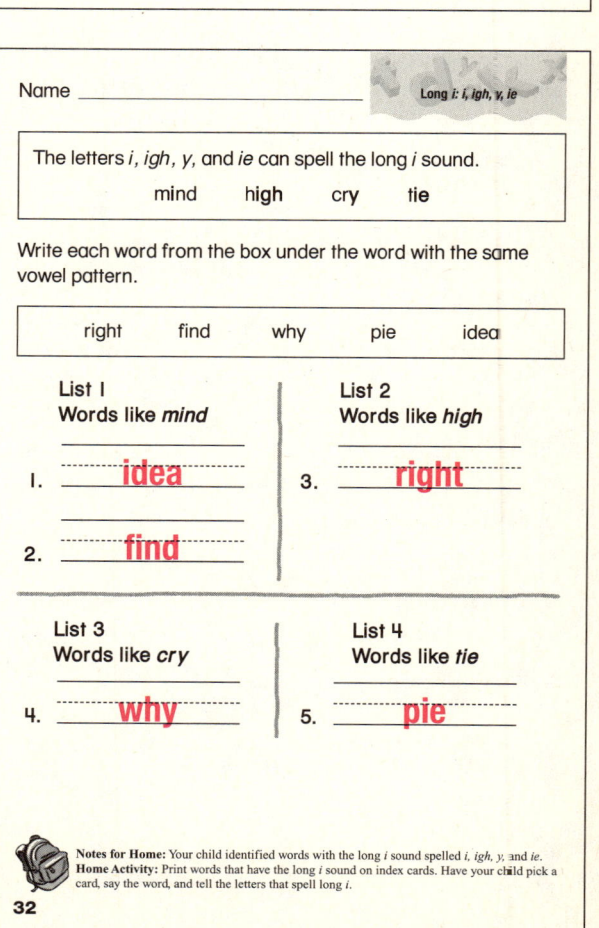

Page 33 — Medial Consonants

Some words have one consonant in the middle: *cabin*.
Some words have two consonants in the middle: *kitten*.

Say each word. Write the number 1 or 2 to tell how many consonants are in the middle of the word. Then write the words that have two middle consonants.

1. wagon — 1
2. follow — 2 — **follow**
3. bottom — 2 — **bottom**
4. tunnel — 2
5. metal — 1
6. dresser — 2 — **tunnel** — **dresser**
7. pillow — 2
8. water — 1
9. butter — 2 — **pillow** — **butter**
10. lizard — 1
11. hippo — 2
12. puppy — 2 — **hippo** — **puppy**
13. tiger — 1
14. river — 1
15. yogurt — 1

Page 34 — Review Long *a*: *a, ai, ay*

The letter *a* can stand for the long *a* sound: *paper*.
The letters *ai* can stand for the long *a* sound: *mail*.
The letters *ay* can stand for the long *a* sound: *day*.

Read the clue by each picture. Draw a line to the word that tells about the picture and has the long *a* sound.

1. follows an animal — tail
2. a place to eat — table
3. month for flowers — May
4. goes with a hammer — nail
5. makes things wet — spray

(Other words: home, saw, water, June, wagon)

Page 35 — Review Inflected Endings -es, -ing, and -s

Words like *reach*, *bark*, and *sleep* do not change their spelling when -es, -ing, or -s is added.
reach—reach**es**   bark—bark**ing**   sleep—sleep**s**

Unscramble each word and write the correct word.

1. Pedro **writes** a letter to a friend. (estwri)
2. Liz looks both ways before she **crosses** the street. (ssesorc)
3. Sam **blows** out the candle. (swobl)
4. The barber **cuts** Pete's hair. (tucs)
5. Jana is **marching** in the parade. (gnrachim)

Page 36 — r-Controlled Vowels: *er, ir, ur*

The letters *er*, *ir*, and *ur* stand for the vowel sound in these words.
h**er**   f**ir**st   t**ur**n

Say each picture name. Circle the word that names the picture. Write the word and circle the letters that stand for the vowel-r sound.

1. hut   huge   (turtle) — t(ur)tle
2. (dirt)   skirt   set — d(ir)t
3. desk   germ   (clerk) — cl(er)k
4. burn   (purse)   prune — p(ur)se
5. first   (stir)   five — st(ir)

Name _____ r-Controlled Vowels: er, ir, ur

The vowel sound in *perch*, *skirt*, and *nurse* is spelled *er*, *ir*, and *ur*.

Find words in the box to complete the puzzle.

| perk | dirt | serve | perch |
| thirsty | burn | purse | fir |

Across
2. needing a drink of water
5. small bag

Down
1. evergreen tree
3. offer food to
4. bird's resting place

Notes for Home: Your child used words with *r*-controlled vowels to complete a crossword puzzle. **Home Activity:** Have your child cut out magazine pictures whose names contain *r*-controlled vowels *(germs, clerk, herd, dirt, fir, shirt, skirt, bird, burn, fur).*

37

Name _____ Plurals -s and -es

To form the plural of many words, add *-s*. To form the plural of words that end in *ch*, *sh*, *s*, *ss*, or *x*, add *-es*. To form the plural of words that end in a consonant and *y*, change the *y* to *i* before adding *-es*.

Each picture shows two or more of something. Read the word and write the plural form of the word.

1. letter  **letters**
2. pony  **ponies**
3. glass  **glasses**
4. fox  **foxes**
5. puppy  **puppies**

Notes for Home: Your child formed the plural of words by adding *-s* or *-es* to the base word. **Home Activity:** Have your child look through advertisements and list plural words. Encourage your child to underline the letters that are used to form each plural.

38

Name _____ Review Long *i*: *i*, *igh*, *y*, and *ie*

Words like *tiger*, *sign*, *try*, and *lie* have the long *i* sound spelled *i*, *igh*, *y*, and *ie*.

Name the picture. Write the word with the long *i* sound to complete the phrase.

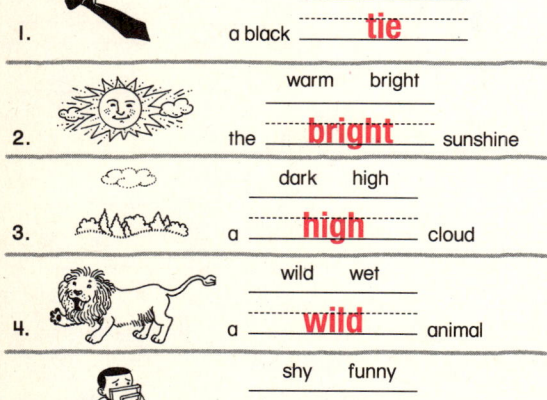

1. a black ___**tie**___ (tie pit)
2. the ___**bright**___ sunshine (warm bright)
3. a ___**high**___ cloud (dark high)
4. a ___**wild**___ animal (wild wet)
5. a ___**shy**___ student (shy funny)

Notes for Home: Your child identified words with the long *i* sound spelled *i*, *igh*, *y*, and *ie*. **Home Activity:** Have your child make a list of words in which the long *i* vowel sound is spelled *i*, *igh*, *y*, or *ie*.

39

Name _____ Review Medial Consonants

Yogurt and *spider* have one consonant in the middle. *Paddle* and *rattle* have double consonants in the middle.

Circle the word that completes the sentence. Write each circled word in the correct list.

1. The ___ slept near the fireplace. kennel (kitten)
2. The dog liked to ride in the ___. (wagon) waffle
3. Drop the ___ in the mailbox. lever (letter)
4. The clown made the girl ___. gobble (giggle)
5. Our ___ is near a lake. (cabin) copper

Double consonants
kitten
letter
giggle

Single consonants
wagon
cabin

Notes for Home: Your child identified words with one or two consonants in the middle. **Home Activity:** Help your child think of other words with one or two middle consonants and list them on a sheet of paper.

40

---

160 Answers

Page 41

Long o: o, oa, ow, oe

The long o sound can be spelled with the letters o, oa, ow, or oe.

only   float   grow   hoe

Look at each picture. Write the long o word for the picture.

1. toe
2. snow
3. boat
4. goat
5. bowl
6. robot
7. bow
8. gold
9. toast
10. mow

Notes for Home: Your child identified words with the long o sound spelled o, oa, ow, or oe. **Home Activity:** Have your child write a sentence using four words from this page and draw a picture to go with the sentence.

Page 42

Long o: o, oa, ow, oe

The long o sound can be spelled with the letters o, oa, ow, or oe.

go   toad   slow   toe

Write the words that have the long o sound inside the giant o.

road	low	blow	load
hop	foam	box	clock
goal	top	no	lock
told	fox	only	hoe

road, low, blow, load, foam, goal, no, told, only, hoe

Notes for Home: Your child identified words with the long o sound spelled o, oa, ow, or oe. **Home Activity:** Have your child write sentences about a boat trip using the words boat, float, slow, old, and row.

Page 43

Compound Words

A compound word is a word made up of two smaller words.

air + plane = airplane   birth + day = birthday

Circle each compound word. Write the compound words.

1. teacher
2. (baseball)
3. animal
4. (afternoon)
5. pencil
6. (anyone)
7. sentence
8. (sidewalk)
9. (outside)
10. person
11. (doorbell)
12. question
13. (doghouse)
14. (notebook)
15. tiger

baseball   afternoon   anyone
sidewalk   outside   doorbell
doghouse   notebook

Notes for Home: Your child identified compound words. **Home Activity:** Write the words down, town, rain, drop, sun, shine, bed, room, every, thing, my, and self on cards and have your child put the cards together to make compound words.

Page 44

Review r-Controlled Vowels: er, ir, ur

The letters er, ir, and ur stand for the same vowel sound.

p**er**k   g**ir**l   h**ur**t

Write a word from the box to complete each tongue twister. Then underline the letters that stand for the vowel sound.

| perch | dirt | fir | turn | serve |

1. Sandy will _____ salad in a seashell.   s**er**ve
2. Please put Polly Parrot on her _____.   p**er**ch
3. Dale's dog Dixie dug deep in the _____.   d**ir**t
4. It's Tina's _____ to take a trip.   t**ur**n
5. The forest was full of fat _____ trees.   f**ir**

Notes for Home: Your child wrote words with r-controlled vowels. **Home Activity:** Help your child look through a book and find words that have the same vowel sound as girl.

Answers **161**

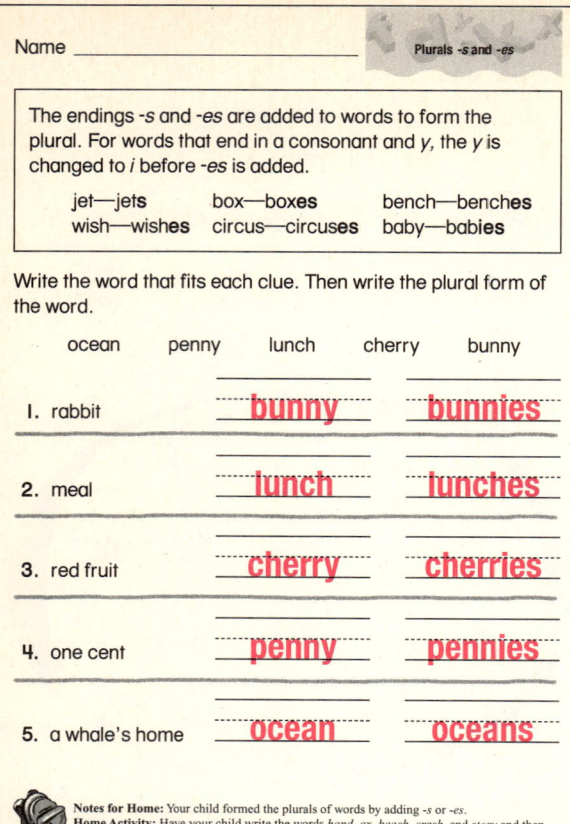

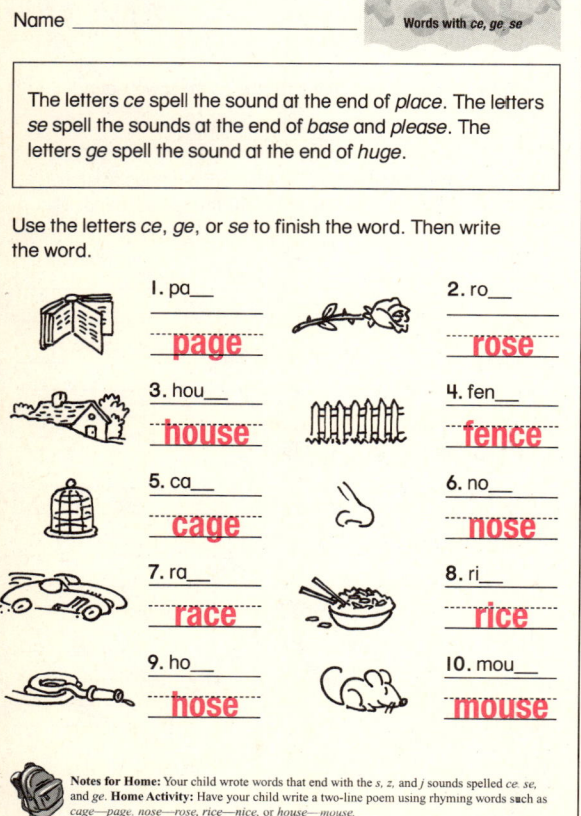

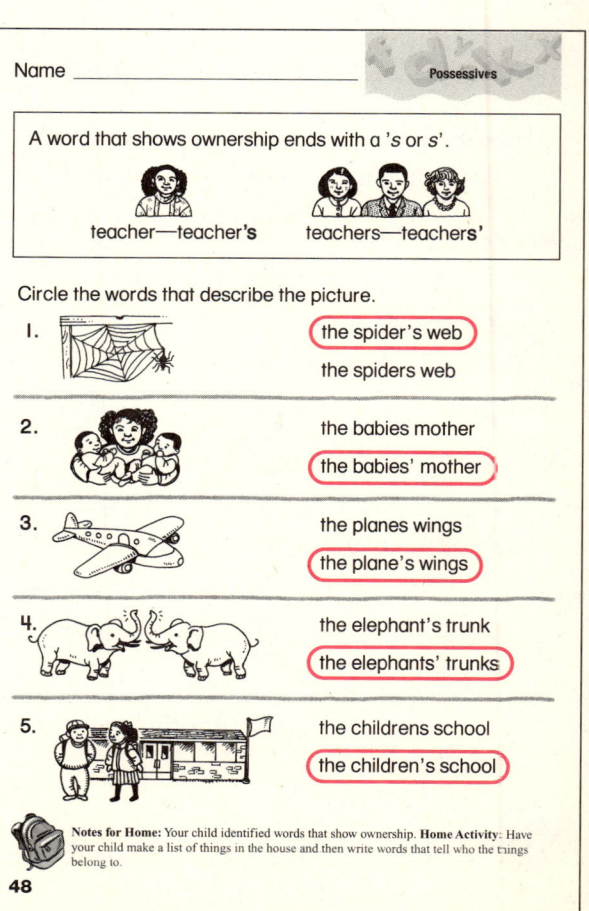

Review Long o: o, oa, ow, oe

The letters *o*, *oa*, *ow*, and *oe* stand for the long *o* vowel sound.

so   boat   own   hoe

Write a word from the list to complete each phrase. Then circle the letters that stand for the long *o* sound.

grow goat show goal float
only throw blow toe cold

1. **throw** a ball
2. scored a **goal**
3. an **only** child
4. stubbed her **toe**
5. a **cold** winter day

Notes for Home: Your child identified words with the long *o* sound spelled *o*, *oa*, *ow*, or *oe*. **Home Activity:** Have your child choose a word from the page and think of a word that rhymes with it.

49

Compound Words

Two smaller words put together make a compound word.
side + walk = sidewalk   any + thing = anything

Write the two words that make up each compound word.

1. raincoat = **rain** + **coat**
2. doghouse = **dog** + **house**
3. mailbox = **mail** + **box**
4. cookbook = **cook** + **book**
5. bedroom = **bed** + **room**

Notes for Home: Your child identified words that make up compound words. **Home Activity:** Have your child use each compound word in a sentence.

50

Vowel Diphthongs ou, ow

The letters *ou* stand for the vowel sound in *out*.
The letters *ow* stand for the vowel sound in *down*.

Circle the word in each row that has the same vowel sound as *out* and *down*.

1. rope   clock   **cow**
2. **mouse**   pop   soap
3. **frown**   cot   rose
4. hole   cob   **found**
5. block   **crown**   smoke
6. **pound**   born   hose
7. **bounce** note   hot
8. float   **ground** mop
9. dog   lock   **south**
10. **brown**   mom   nose

Notes for Home: Your child identified words with the vowel sound in *out*. **Home Activity:** Have your child write four sentences using *ou* and *ow* words from this page.

51

Vowel Diphthongs ou, ow

The letters *ou* and *ow* stand for the vowel sound in *count* and *cow*.

Choose the letters *ou* or *ow* to finish each word. Write the word.

1. We watched the funny cl____n. **clown**
2. The s____nd of thunder woke me up. **sound**
3. The baby kangaroo hid in the p____ch. **pouch**
4. The unhappy boy had a fr____n on his face. **frown**
5. Use a t____el to dry the dishes. **towel**

Notes for Home: Your child wrote *ou* and *ow* words. **Home Activity:** Have your child use *ou* and *ow* words to tell a story about a mouse going to town.

52

Inflected Endings

When a word ends with one vowel followed by one consonant, the final consonant is doubled before -ed or -ing is added.

drip—dripp**ed**   hug—hugg**ing**

Follow the signs to make a new word. Write the word.

1. trip + ed — **tripped**
2. swim + ing — **swimming**
3. stop + ing — **stopping**
4. run + ing — **running**
5. pat + ed — **patted**
6. mop + ed — **mopped**
7. let + ing — **letting**
8. shrug + ed — **shrugged**
9. hop + ed — **hopped**
10. bat + ing — **batting**

Notes for Home: Your child doubled the final consonant in words before adding -ed and -ing. **Home Activity:** Have your child write five sentences using words from this page.

53

Words with ce, ge, se

The letters ce and se spell the sound at the end of race and mouse. The letters se can also spell the sound at the end of tease. The letters ge spell the sound at the end of cage.

Find five words in the puzzle that end with ce, ge, or se. Circle each word in the puzzle. Then write the word.

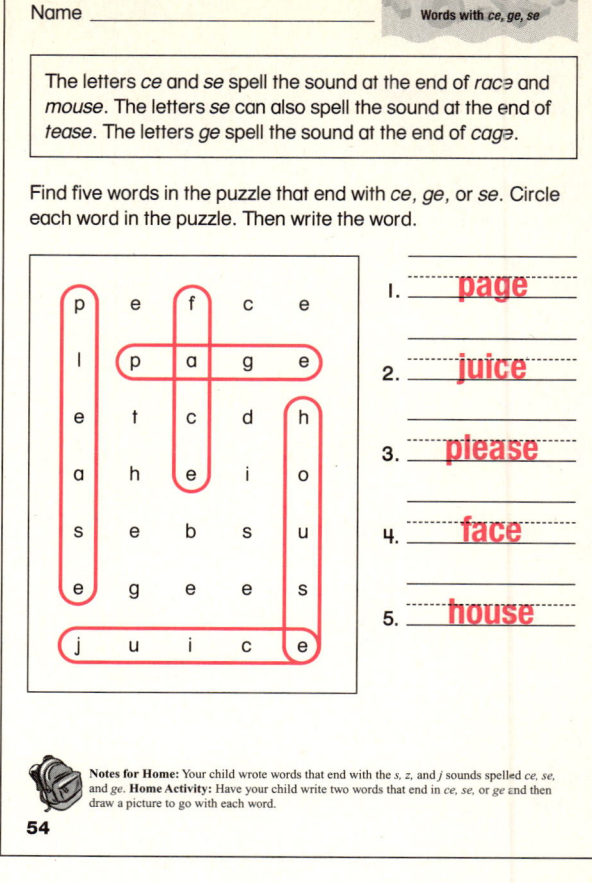

1. **page**
2. **juice**
3. **please**
4. **face**
5. **house**

Notes for Home: Your child wrote words that end with the s, z, and j sounds spelled ce, se, and ge. **Home Activity:** Have your child write two words that end in ce, se, or ge and then draw a picture to go with each word.

54

Review Possessives

A possessive word ends with 's or s'.

Betty**'s** book   the girl**s'** shoes

Add 's or s' to the underlined word to show ownership.

1. the desks of the students
   the **students'** desks
2. the book of Miguel
   Miguel's book
3. the buttons of the shirt
   the **shirt's** buttons
4. the playground of the school
   the **school's** playground
5. the uniforms of the players
   the **players'** uniforms

Notes for Home: Your child added 's or s' to words to show ownership. **Home Activity:** Write the names of familiar people and objects on one side of cards and have your child write the possessive forms of the words on the other side.

55

---

r-Controlled Vowel: ar

The letters ar stand for the vowel sound in card.

Circle the word that completes each sentence and has the same vowel sound as card. Write the word.

1. The kitten plays with ____.
   (yarn)   me   **yarn**
2. Uncle Lin bought a new ____.
   bike   (car)   **car**
3. We saw a ____ in the ocean.
   (shark)   whale   **shark**
4. The band will ____.
   play   (march)   **march**
5. Put the marbles in a ____.
   (jar)   sack   **jar**

Notes for Home: Your child wrote ar words to complete sentences. **Home Activity:** Have your child write a sentence for each ar word on the page.

56

---

164 Answers

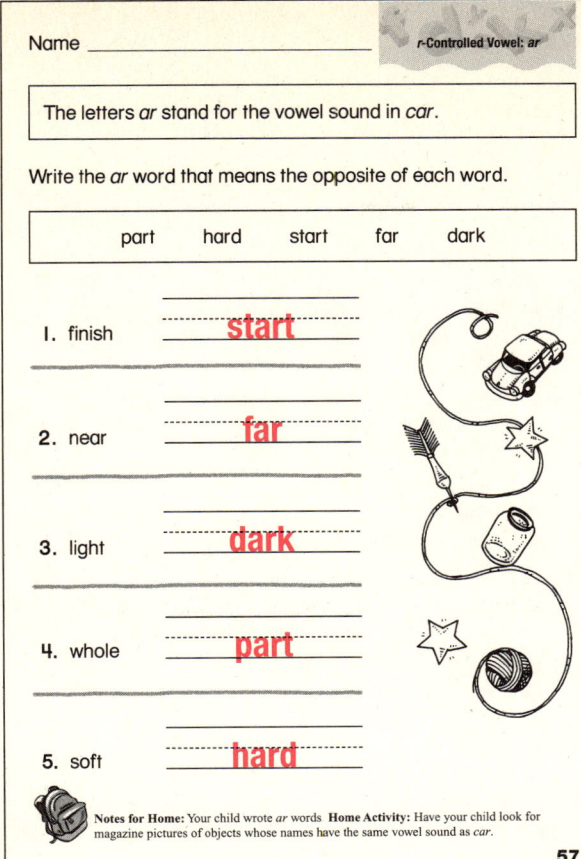

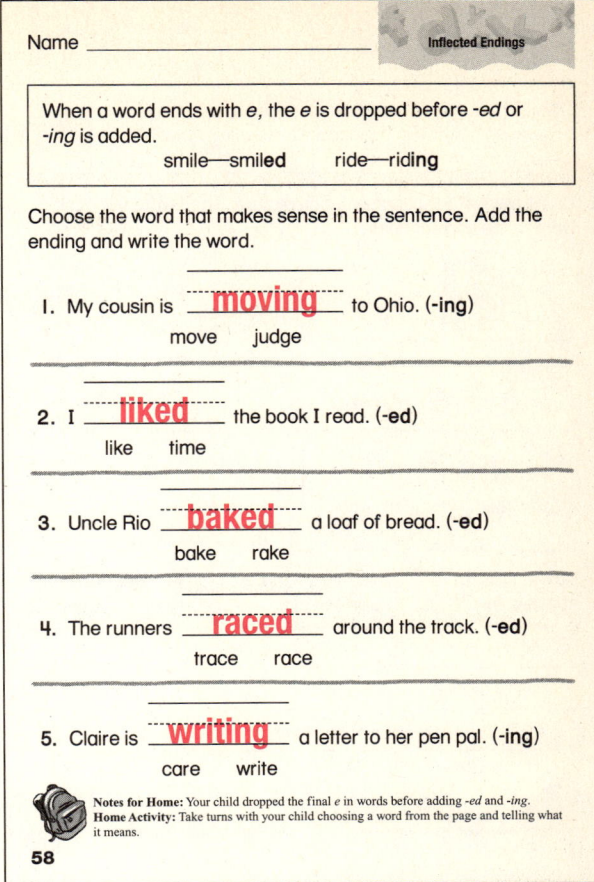

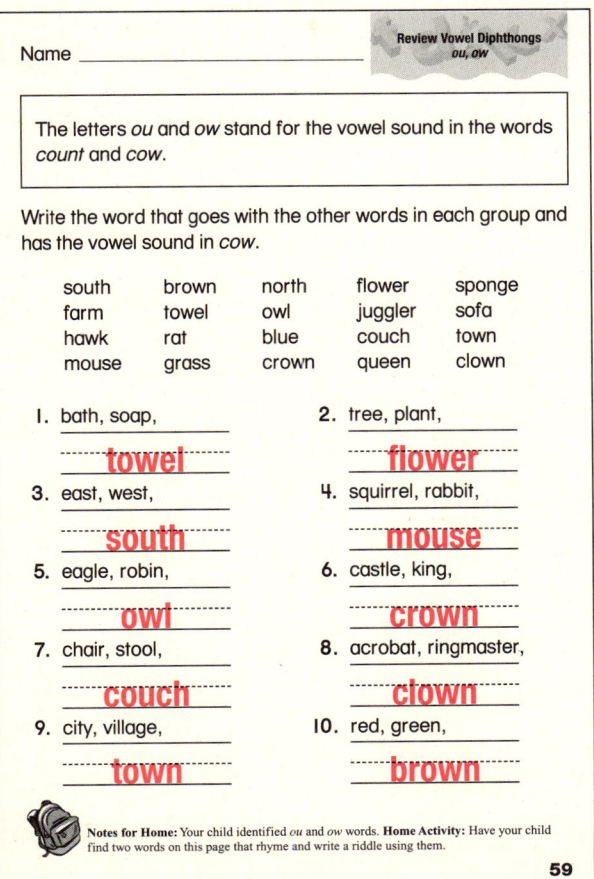

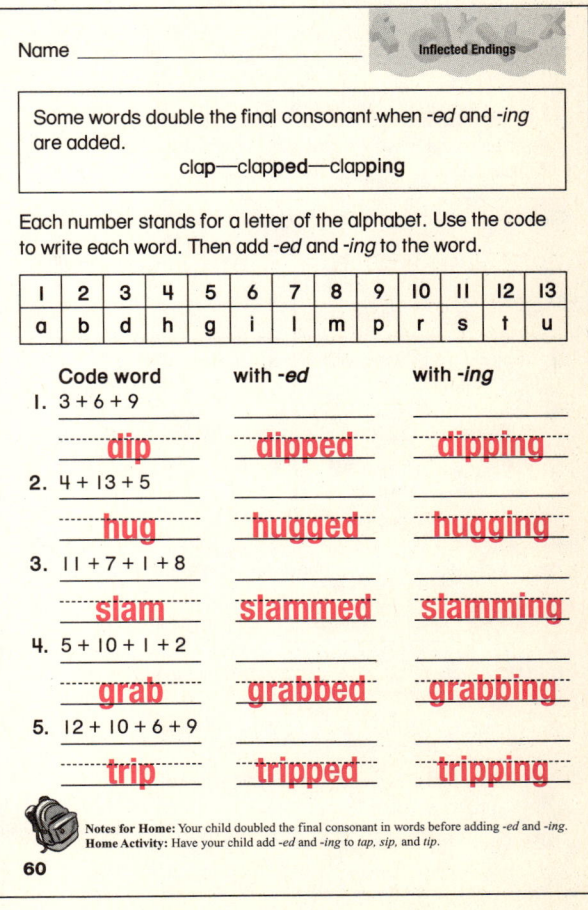

Answers **165**

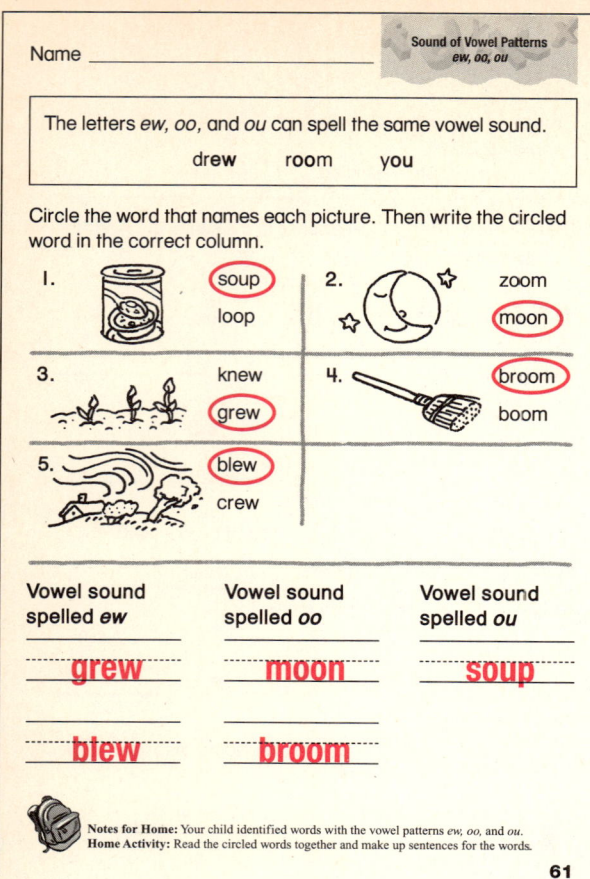
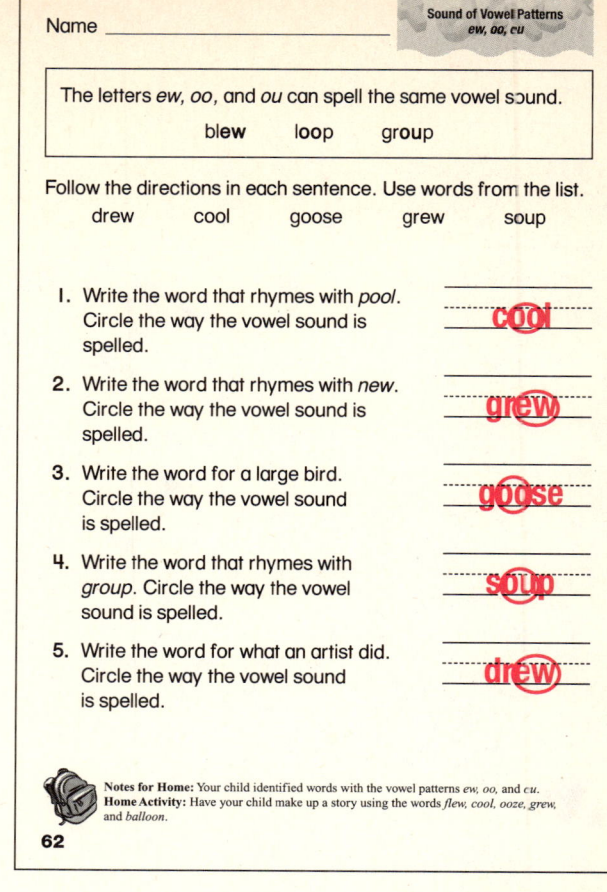
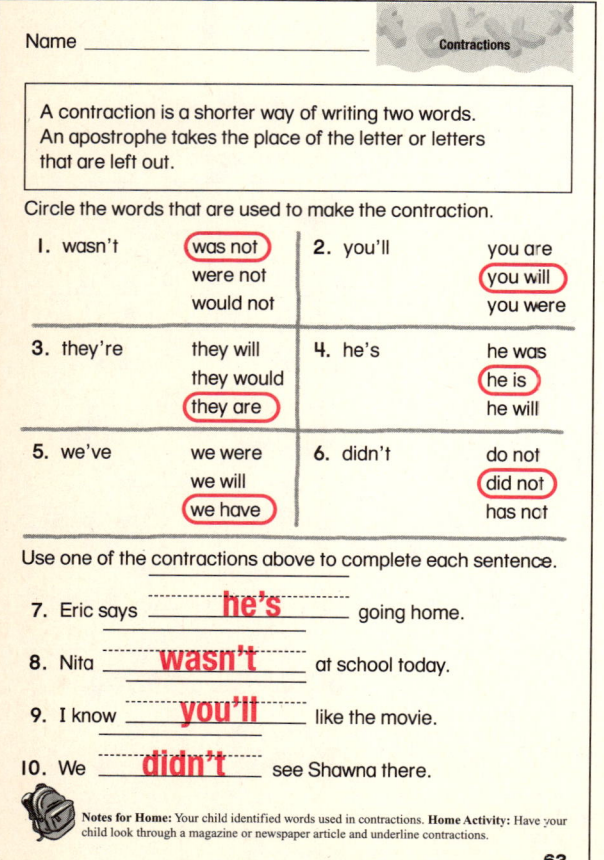
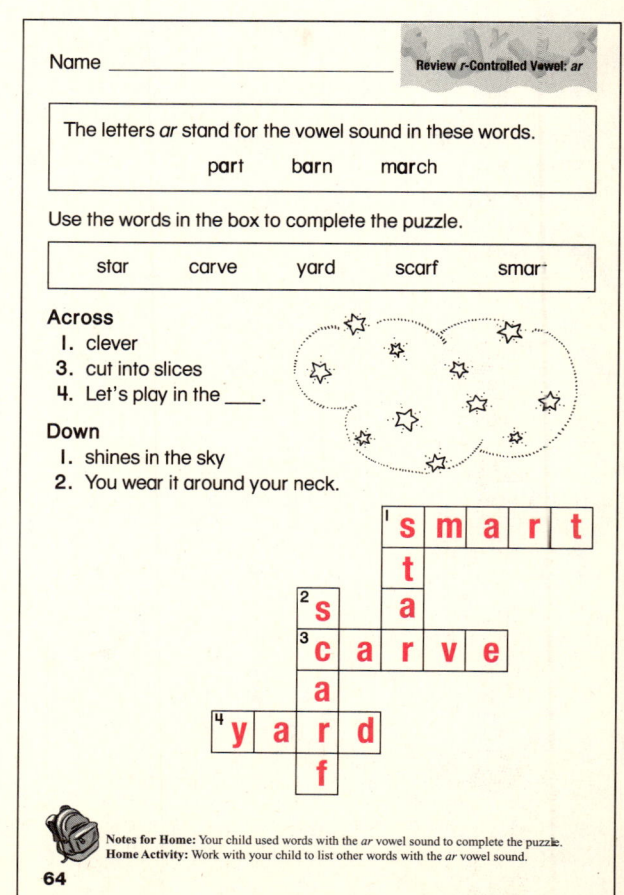

166 Answers

Page 65

Inflected Endings

When a word ends in *e*, the *e* is dropped before *-ed* or *-ing* is added.

care—car**ed**   hike—hik**ing**

Write each word. Then write the word with *-ed* and *-ing*.

| rake | smile | trace | like | skate |

Word	Add -ed	Add -ing
1. rake	raked	raking
2. smile	smiled	smiling
3. trace	traced	tracing
4. like	liked	liking
5. skate	skated	skating

Notes for Home: Your child dropped the final *e* in words before adding *-ed* and *-ing*. **Home Activity:** Look through a newspaper together to find words that follow this pattern. Make a list of the words.

Page 66

r-Controlled Vowels: or, ore, oor, our

Read the words and listen for the vowel sound.

h**or**n   m**ore**   fl**oor**   f**our**

Write the *r*-controlled vowel word used in each sentence.

1. She will pour the water. — **pour**
2. It is cooler on the porch. — **porch**
3. Joel knocked on the front door. — **door**
4. The score of the game was 6 to 3. — **score**
5. The horse ran through the meadow. — **horse**

Notes for Home: Your child identified words with the *or, ore, oor,* and *our* vowel patterns. **Home Activity:** Write the letters *or, ore, oor,* and *our* on paper and help your child write other words with these vowel patterns.

Page 67

r-Controlled Vowels: or, ore, oor, our

The letters *or, ore, oor,* and *our* stand for the vowel sound in these words.

c**or**n   t**ore**   d**oor**   f**our**

Write the word that answers the question. Draw a line under the letters that stand for the vowel sound.

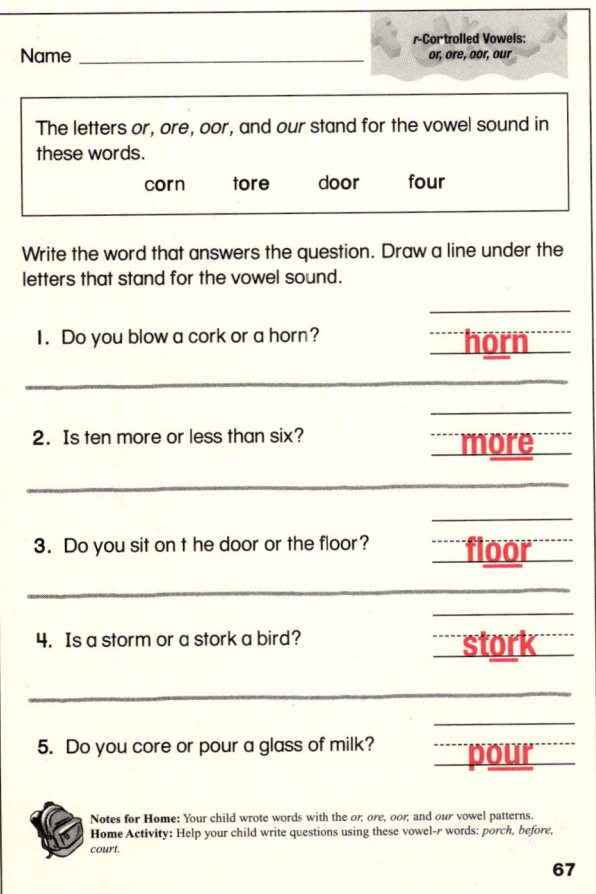

1. Do you blow a cork or a horn? — **horn**
2. Is ten more or less than six? — **more**
3. Do you sit on the door or the floor? — **floor**
4. Is a storm or a stork a bird? — **stork**
5. Do you core or pour a glass of milk? — **pour**

Notes for Home: Your child wrote words with the *or, ore, oor,* and *our* vowel patterns. **Home Activity:** Help your child write questions using these vowel-*r* words: *porch, before, court.*

Page 68

Inflected Endings

If the base word ends in *y*, the *y* is changed to *i* before *-ed* or *-es* is added.
If the base word ends in *y*, the *y* stays when *-ing* is added.

carry—carr**ies**—carr**ied**—carry**ing**

Write each word from the box under the heading that tells what happens to the base word when *-ed, -es,* or *-ing* is added.

| hurries | crying | dried | worrying | tries |
| fried | trying | prying | drying | supplied |

No change	Change y to i
1. crying	6. hurries
2. worrying	7. dried
3. trying	8. tries
4. prying	9. fried
5. drying	10. supplied

Notes for Home: Your child identified words in which the spelling changes before *-ed* or *-es* is added. **Home Activity:** Have your child write the base words for the words on this page.

Review Sound of Vowel Patterns ew, oo, ou

The letters *ew*, *oo*, and *ou* can spell the same vowel sound.
n**ew**   z**oo**m   gr**ou**p

Write the word that matches each clue. Draw a line under the letters that stand for the vowel sound in the word.

| you | soup | stool | drew | spoons |

1. food made by boiling vegetables or meat — s**ou**p
2. eating tools — sp**oo**ns
3. something to sit on — st**oo**l
4. made a picture — dr**ew**
5. the person spoken to — y**ou**

Notes for Home: Your child wrote words with the vowel patterns *ew*, *oo*, and *ou*.
Home Activity: Help your child write a rhyming word for each word on this page.

69

Contractions

An apostrophe (') takes the place of the letter or letters that are left out when two smaller words are written as a contraction.
do not—don't

Write the contraction for the underlined words in each sentence.

1. Leah says <u>she is</u> going home. — she's
2. <u>You are</u> late for dinner. — You're
3. <u>We have</u> been playing basketball. — We've
4. Iyo <u>did not</u> water the plants. — didn't
5. <u>I will</u> meet you at the library. — I'll

Notes for Home: Your child has written two smaller words as contractions.
Home Activity: Help your child make a list of contractions.

70

Sound of Vowel Patterns oo, ou

The letters *oo* and *ou* stand for the same vowel sound in these words.
l**oo**k   c**ou**ld

Circle each word that has the same vowel sound as the picture name.

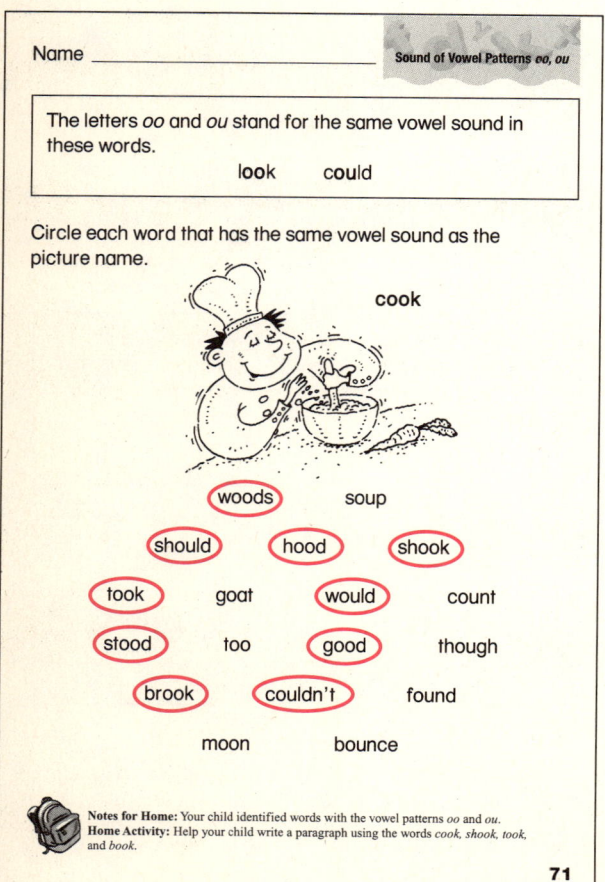

cook

(woods)   soup
(should)   (hood)   (shook)
(took)   goat   (would)   count
(stood)   too   (good)   though
(brook)   (couldn't)   found
moon   bounce

Notes for Home: Your child identified words with the vowel patterns *oo* and *ou*.
Home Activity: Help your child write a paragraph using the words *cook*, *shook*, *took*, and *book*.

71

Sound of Vowel Patterns oo, ou

The letters *oo* and *ou* stand for the vowel sound in these words.
t**oo**k   c**ou**ld

Write the word that has the same vowel sound as the first word in the row.

hood   1. school   book   room — book
should 2. around   couldn't   dough — couldn't
cook   3. woods   zoom   tooth — woods
good   4. wouldn't   you   tool — wouldn't
foot   5. flour   brook   pool — brook

Notes for Home: Your child identified words with the vowel patterns *oo* and *ou*.
Home Activity: Have your child write a book title using one word with the *oo* vowel pattern and one word with the *ou* vowel pattern.

72

© Scott Foresman 2

168 Answers

Page 73 — Comparative Endings -er, -est

To compare two things, -er is added to the base word.
To compare three or more things, -est is added to the base word.

big—big**er** than you   little—little**st** of all

Add -er or -est to the base word to complete each phrase.

1. wise — **wiser** than an owl
2. fat — **fattest** of all the puppies
3. hot — **hotter** than last summer
4. tall — **tallest** of the buildings
5. large — **largest** house on the street

Notes for Home: Your child used words with -er and -est endings to make comparisons.
Home Activity: Have your child gather household objects and compare them using *little, new,* and *big* with -er and -est endings.

Page 74 — Review r-Controlled Vowels: or, ore, oor, our

The letters *or, ore, oor,* and *our* stand for the vowel sound in these words.

corn   sore   door   pour

Write each word in the correct box.

horn   before   court   pork   born
four   floor   tore   north more

or
1. horn
2. pork
3. born
4. north

ore
6. before
7. tore
8. more

oor
5. floor

our
9. court
10. four

Notes for Home: Your child wrote words with the r-controlled vowels *or, ore, oor,* and *our.*
Home Activity: Have your child choose five words from this page and write a sentence using each word.

Page 75 — Inflected Endings

The *y* is changed to *i* before -es and -ed is added if the base word ends in *y.*
The *y* is kept when -ing is added if the base word ends in *y.*

dry   dries   dried   drying

Add -ed to each word. Write the word.
1. try — **tried**
2. pry — **pried**
3. marry — **married**
4. reply — **replied**

Add -es to each word. Write the word.
5. fry — **fries**
6. cry — **cries**
7. carry — **carries**
8. worry — **worries**

Add -ing to each word. Write the word.
9. fly — **flying**
10. hurry — **hurrying**

Notes for Home: Your child changed the spelling of base words before adding -ed or -es.
Home Activity: Have your child choose four words from this page and write a sentence using each one.

Page 76 — r-Controlled Vowels: ear, eer

The letters *ear* and *eer* stand for the vowel sound in these words.

n**ear**   d**eer**

Underline the words in the box that have the same vowel sound as *near* and *deer.* Then write each underlined word next to its meaning.

clear   read   break   **year**   **beard**
cheer   leather   head   **steer**   great

1. twelve months — **year**
2. grows on the chin — **beard**
3. an animal — **steer**
4. shout or yell — **cheer**
5. can see through — **clear**

Notes for Home: Your child identified words with the r-controlled vowels *ear* and *eer.*
Home Activity: Work together with your child and make up sentences using the words he or she wrote.

Answers **169**

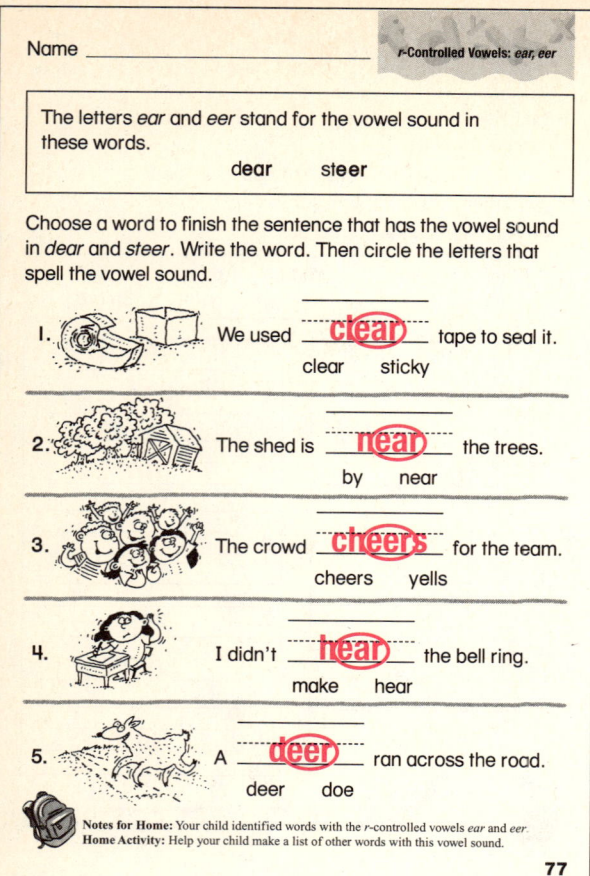

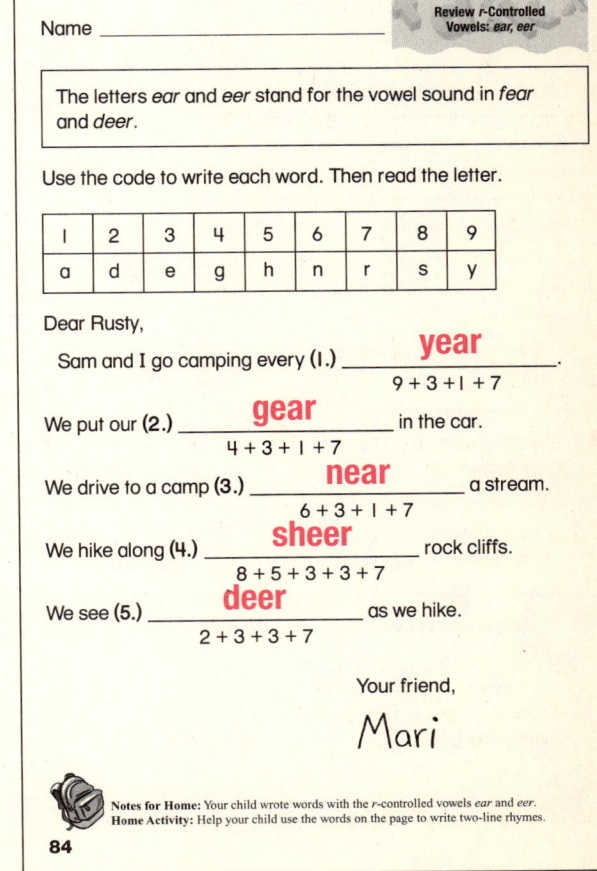

Review Suffix -ly

The suffix -ly can be added to a base word to make a new word.
quick—quick**ly**   pretty—pretti**ly**

Choose a word from the box to answer each clue. Add -ly to the base word and write the word. Some words can answer more than one clue.

| swift | quiet | sad | happy | slow |

1. how the children played in the park — **happily**
2. how a fox runs — **swiftly**
3. how the boy spoke in the library — **quietly**
4. how the girl looked at her broken doll — **sadly**
5. how a turtle moves — **slowly**

Notes for Home: Your child added the suffix -ly to base words. Home Activity: Have your child choose three -ly words from the page and write a sentence for each word.

85

Short e: ea

The word *ready* has the short *e* sound spelled with the letters *ea*.

Say the two picture names. Write the word that has the short *e* vowel sound spelled *ea* as in *ready*.

1. **thread**
2. **head**
3. **heavy**
4. **feather**
5. **sweater**

Notes for Home: Your child identified words with the short *e* vowel sound spelled *ea*. Home Activity: Together make up a sentence for each picture name with the short *e* vowel sound.

86

Short e: ea

The short *e* sound can be spelled *ea*.

Underline the words with the same vowel sound as *ready*. Then follow the directions.

treasure	great	dead	steak	wealth
breakfast	weather	break	bread	head
real	sweater	leave	heavy	meadow

1. Write the word that names a meal. — **breakfast**
2. Write the word that rhymes with *feather*. — **weather**
3. Write the word that means a great deal of money. — **wealth**
4. Write the word that names something to eat. — **bread**
5. Write the word that names part of the body. — **head**

Notes for Home: Your child identified words with the short *e* vowel sound spelled *ea*. Home Activity: Look through a newspaper together to find words with short *e* spelled *ea*.

87

Suffix -er

When you add the suffix -er to a word, you make a new word that means a person or thing that does something.
bake—bak**er**   jog—jog**ger**

Add -er to the word that tells about the picture. Write the new word.

1. play / paint — **painter**
2. help / farm — **farmer**
3. work / dance — **dancer**
4. skate / run — **skater**
5. mix / clean — **mixer**

Notes for Home: Your child added the suffix -er to make new words. Home Activity: Together add -er to the other words on the page.

88

© Scott Foresman 2

172   Answers

Page 89 — Review Vowel Diphthongs *oi, oy*

The letters *oi* and *oy* stand for the vowel sound in the words *foil* and *toy*.

Choose a word from the box that can replace the underlined word or words in each sentence. Write the word.

| moist | boil | boy | joy | soil |

1. We planted seeds in the <u>dirt</u>. — **soil**
2. Saad washed his face with a <u>wet</u> cloth. — **moist**
3. The <u>young man</u> rode his bike to school. — **boy**
4. The water in the pot began to <u>cook rapidly</u>. — **boil**
5. Her heart was filled with <u>happiness</u>. — **joy**

Page 90 — Review Suffix *-ful*

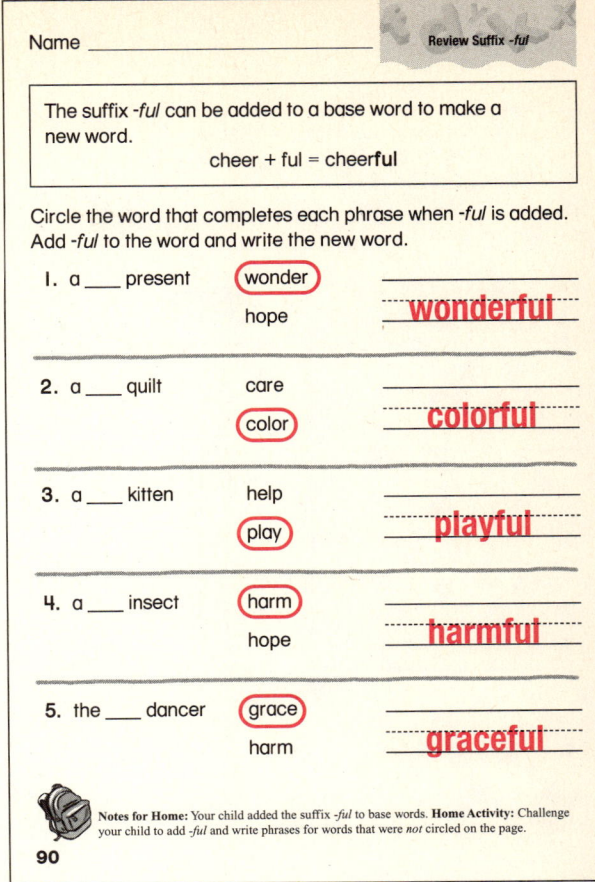

The suffix *-ful* can be added to a base word to make a new word.
    cheer + ful = cheer**ful**

Circle the word that completes each phrase when *-ful* is added. Add *-ful* to the word and write the new word.

1. a ___ present — (wonder) / hope — **wonderful**
2. a ___ quilt — care / (color) — **colorful**
3. a ___ kitten — help / (play) — **playful**
4. a ___ insect — (harm) / hope — **harmful**
5. the ___ dancer — (grace) / harm — **graceful**

Page 91 — /ò/ Vowel Patterns *a, al, au*

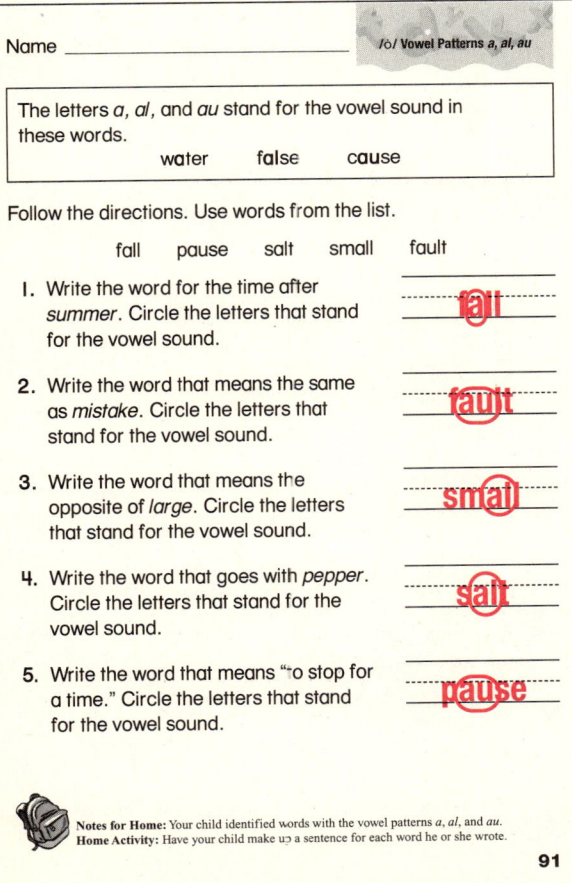

The letters *a*, *al*, and *au* stand for the vowel sound in these words.
    water   false   cause

Follow the directions. Use words from the list.

    fall   pause   salt   small   fault

1. Write the word for the time after *summer*. Circle the letters that stand for the vowel sound. — **fall**
2. Write the word that means the same as *mistake*. Circle the letters that stand for the vowel sound. — **fault**
3. Write the word that means the opposite of *large*. Circle the letters that stand for the vowel sound. — **small**
4. Write the word that goes with *pepper*. Circle the letters that stand for the vowel sound. — **salt**
5. Write the word that means "to stop for a time." Circle the letters that stand for the vowel sound. — **pause**

Page 92 — /ò/ Vowel Patterns *a, al, au*

The words *water*, *walk*, and *cause* have the same vowel sound.
    water   walk   cause

Circle the word that tells about the picture. Write the word.

1. stalk (saucer) — **saucer**
2. false (laundry) — **laundry**
3. (salt) small — **salt**
4. (call) cause — **call**
5. (water) walk — **water**
6. (ball) fault — **ball**
7. false talk — **talk**
8. (faucet) laundry — **faucet**
9. (tall) small — **tall**
10. hall (walnut) — **walnut**

Answers 173

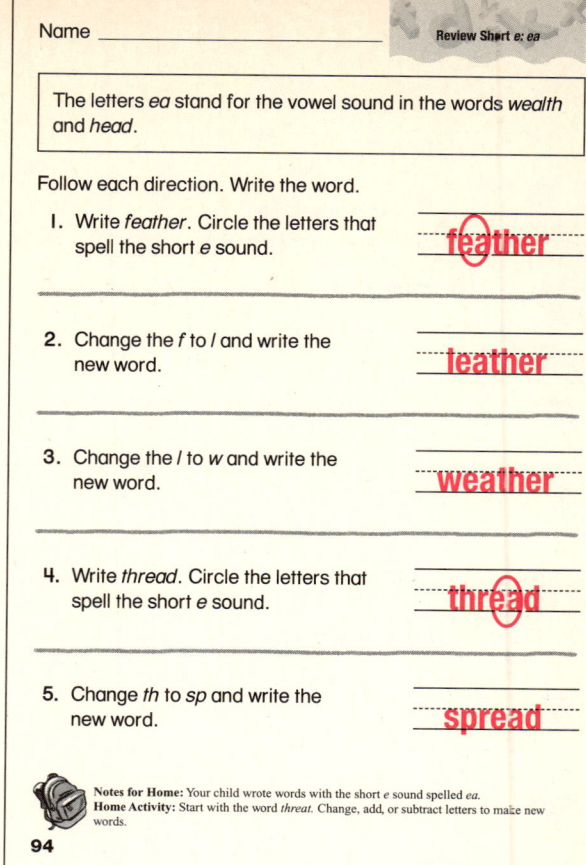

174 Answers

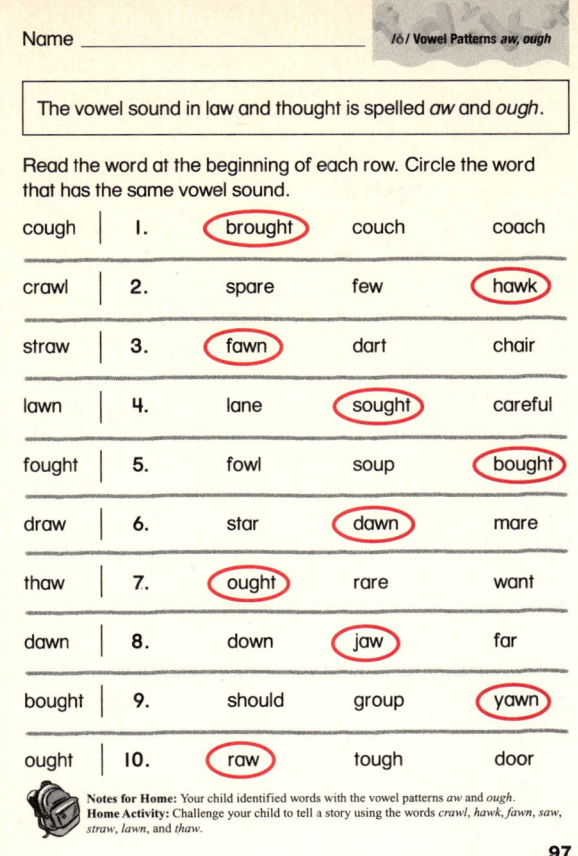
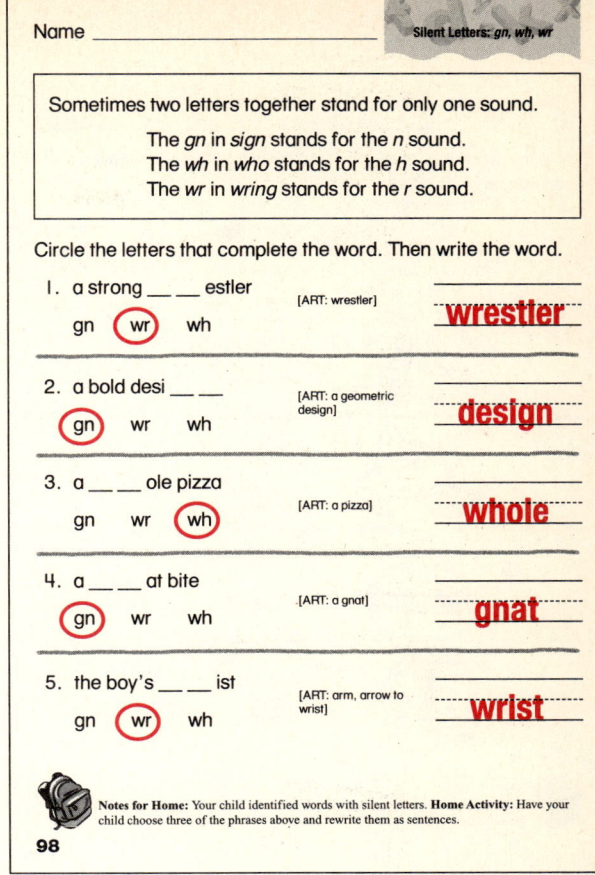
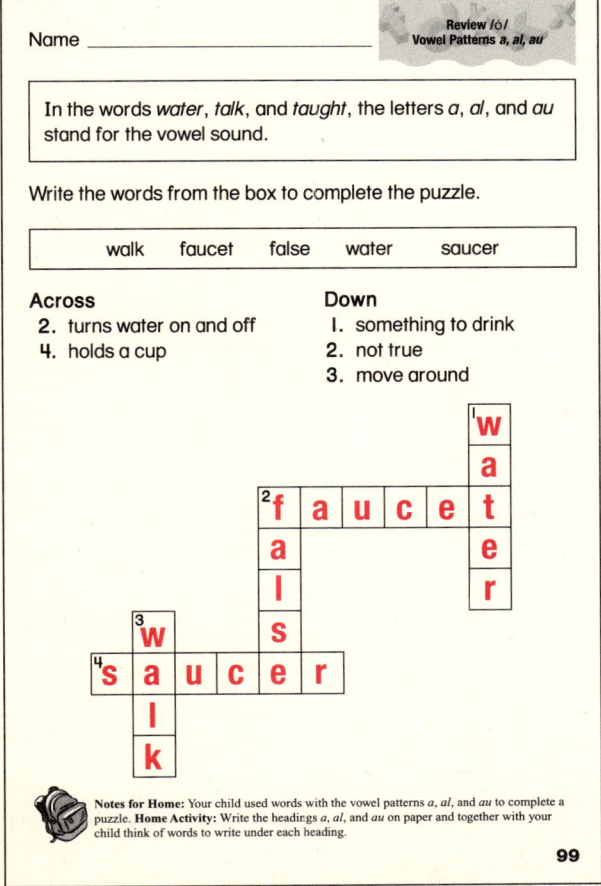
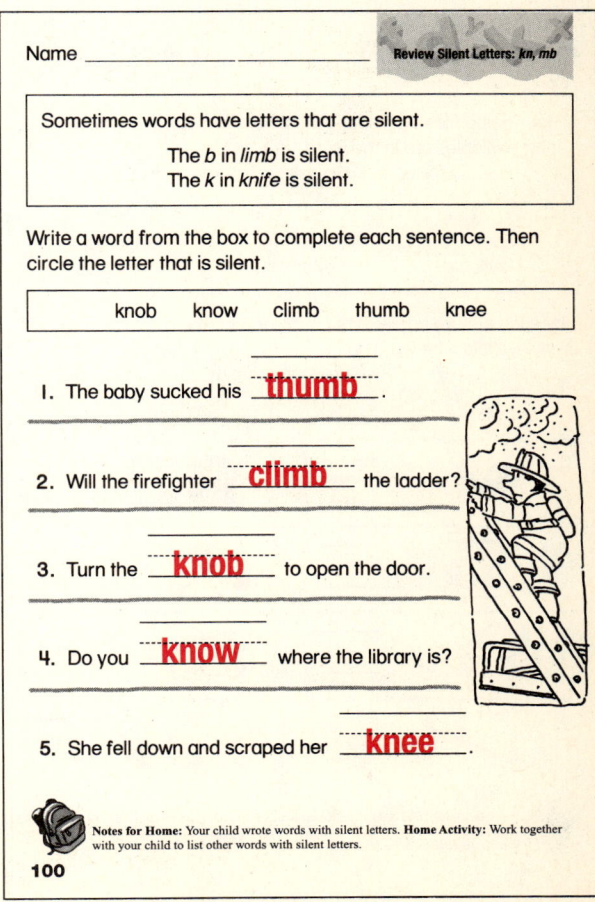

Answers **175**

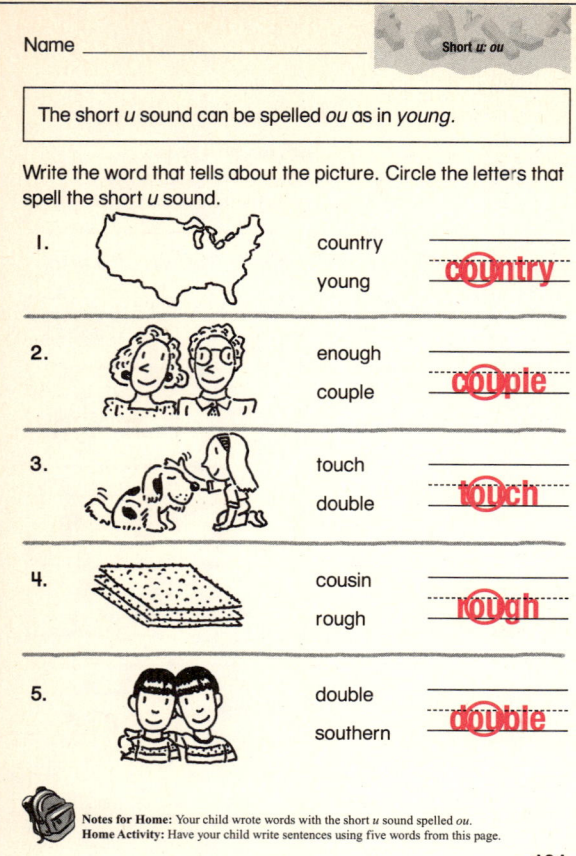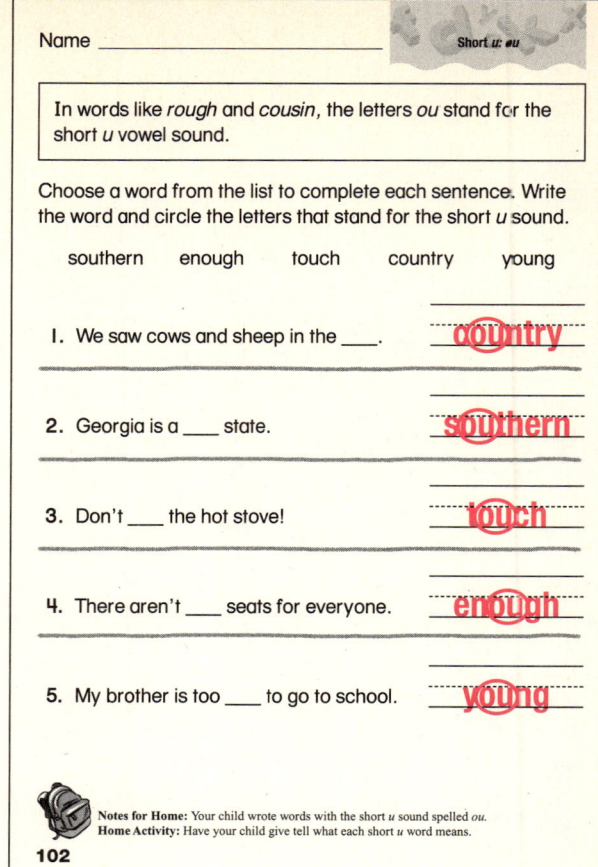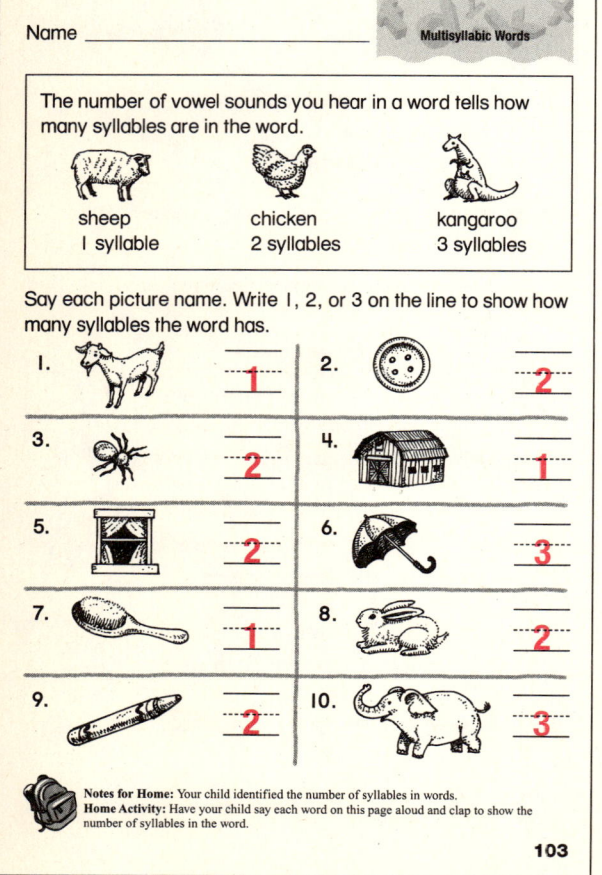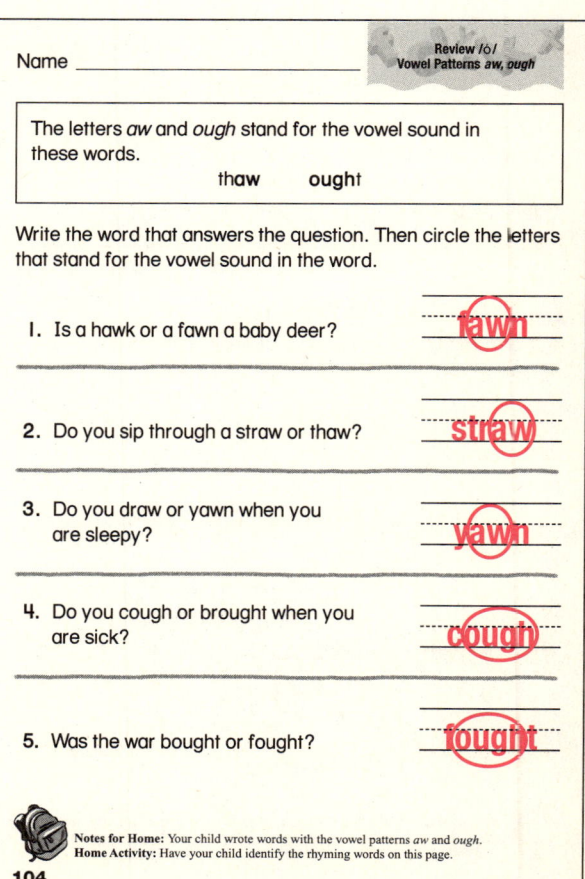

176 Answers

Page 105

Review Silent Letters: gn, wh, wr

In words like *design*, *whom*, and *wrap*, some letters are silent.

Write the word from the box that completes each sentence. Then underline the letter that is silent.

| sign | wrong | wrote | who | gnaw |

1. Rima **wrote** a letter to her cousin.
2. Did you see **who** won the race?
3. The **sign** said "Two for One Sale!"
4. Dogs like to **gnaw** on bones.
5. Something is **wrong** with the computer.

Notes for Home: Your child wrote words with silent letters. **Home Activity:** Have your child write a tongue twister using words with silent letters.

Page 106

Schwa Sound in *across* and *people*

The schwa sound can be spelled *a*.
    across   **a**bout
The schwa sound can be spelled consonant + *le*.
    peo**ple**   hum**ble**

Write the word with the schwa sound to complete each sentence.

1. Yuka lives in the apartment **above** me.
   below   above
2. Erica wore a **purple** sweater.
   green   purple
3. Lions live in a **jungle**.
   jungle   zoo
4. Jorge ran **around** the track.
   around   on
5. The **eagle** soared in the sky.
   hawk   eagle

Notes for Home: Your child wrote words with the schwa sound spelled *a* and consonant + *le*. **Home Activity:** Help your child think of other words with the schwa sound spelled *a* and consonant + *le*.

Page 107

Schwa Sound in *across* and *people*

The schwa sound in *across* is spelled *a*.
The schwa sound in *people* is spelled consonant + *le*.

Circle the word in each sentence that has the schwa sound spelled *a* or consonant + *le*. Write the word.

1. Put your toys (away) before bedtime. — **away**
2. The (kettle) was on the stove. — **kettle**
3. Pat likes to tell (riddles). — **riddles**
4. It is (about) nine o'clock. — **about**
5. The stars seemed to (twinkle). — **twinkle**

Notes for Home: Your child wrote words with the schwa sound spelled *a* and consonant + *le*. **Home Activity:** Have your child underline the letter or letters that stand for the schwa sound in each word he or she wrote.

Page 108

Plural -s and -es

Add *-s* or *-es* to a word to show more than one.
Add *-s* to words like *house*.   house—hous**es**
Add *-es* to words that end in *s*, *ss*, *ch*, *sh*, or *x*.
   ax—ax**es**   church—church**es**
   bush—bush**es**   glass—glass**es**

Write the plural form of the picture name in the sentence.

1. We washed many **dishes**.
2. The park has three **benches**.
3. Two **foxes** slept in the den.
4. The **roses** are beautiful.
5. Several **buses** waited in line.

Notes for Home: Your child added *-s* and *-es* to make the plural forms of words. **Home Activity:** Label two columns *-s* and *-es*. Take turns with your child writing a word and its plural form in each column.

Answers

Name _____ Review Short u: ou

The letters *ou* stand for the short *u* vowel sound in words like *tough*.

The words below have the short *u* sound spelled *ou*. Find and circle each word in the puzzle.

| cousin | enough | southern | couple | trouble |
| touch | rough | country | young | double |

```
e w c o u n t r y r
n e o c o u p l e g
o s y o e t s w y o
u t h u t r a t k t
g h a s d o u b l e
h r s i y u r m h
q o d n h b f b w n
a u f w n l t h a m
c g r a j e y e e u
t h i d o t o u c h
o b s o u t h e r n
y o u n g r g r e s
```

Notes for Home: Your child identified words with the short *u* sound spelled *ou*.
Home Activity: Have your child choose five words and write a sentence for each one.

109

Name _____ Review Multisyllabic Words

Some words have one syllable: *cot, nurse*.
Some words have two syllables: *summer, dentist*.
Some words have three syllables: *umbrella, kangaroo*.

Write 1, 2, or 3 on the line to show how many syllables each word has. Then write the word with two syllables.

1. difficult dime dinner   ___dinner___
   3   **1** **2**

2. bottom   boot bodyguard   ___bottom___
   2   **1** **3**

3. horn   hornet horrible   ___hornet___
   1 **2**   **3**

4. kimono kitten kite   ___kitten___
   3   **2** **1**

5. chain character camel   ___camel___
   1 **3**   **2**

Notes for Home: Your child identified words with one, two, or three syllables.
Home Activity: Have your child look through a magazine and cut out pictures whose names have one, two, or three syllables and sort them according to number of syllables.

110

Name _____ Vowel Digraph *ue*

The letters *ue* stand for the vowel sound in *blue*.

Choose the word from the box that makes sense in the sentence and has the vowel sound in *blue*. Write the word.

| tissue | paste | guard | true | clues |
| hints | statue | handkerchief | glue | real |

1. Bring scissors and ____ to class.   ___glue___

2. Use the ____ to figure out the word's meaning.   ___clues___

3. A ____ stood outside of the building.   ___statue___

4. She wiped her nose with a ____.   ___tissue___

5. The movie was based on a ____ story.   ___true___

Notes for Home: Your child wrote words that have the vowel sound in *blue*.
Home Activity: Take turns with your child choosing a word from the box and making up a sentence for the word.

111

Name _____ Vowel Digraph *ue*

The letters *ue* spell the vowel sound in *blue*.

Follow the directions.

1. Write *blue*. Underline the letters that spell the vowel sound.   ___bl<u>ue</u>___

2. Change *b* to *g*. Write the new word. Underline the letters that spell the vowel sound.   ___gl<u>ue</u>___

3. Change *g* to *c*. Write the new word. Underline the letters that spell the vowel sound.   ___cl<u>ue</u>___

4. Change *cl* to *tr*. Write the new word. Underline the letters that spell the vowel sound.   ___tr<u>ue</u>___

5. Change *tr* to *s*. Write the new word. Underline the letters that spell the vowel sound.   ___s<u>ue</u>___

Notes for Home: Your child wrote words that have the vowel sound in *blue*.
Home Activity: Have your child write a poem using two words from this page.

112

178 Answers

Schwa Sound in *weather*

The schwa sound can be spelled consonant + *er*.
weather   **fev**er

Underline the words that have the schwa sound spelled consonant + *er*. Then follow the directions.

across	hammer	seven	barrel	ladder
dinner	ahead	finger	cabin	water
kitchen	better	feather	beaver	jewel
diet	sweater	muffin	carrot	number

1. Write the word that names an animal that builds dams. — **beaver**
2. Write the word that names 1, 5, 8, 12, 37, or 124. — **number**
3. Write the word that names a tool for hitting. — **hammer**
4. Write the word that names a part of the hand. — **finger**
5. Write the word that names a piece of clothing. — **sweater**

Notes for Home: Your child identified words that have the schwa sound spelled consonant + *er*. **Home Activity:** Together make a list of things around the house whose names have the schwa sound spelled consonant + *er*.

113

Review Schwa Sound in *across* and *people*

The schwa sound can be spelled *a* or consonant + *le*.
along   bri**dle**

Unscramble the letters to make a word that has the schwa sound spelled *a* or consonant + *le* and that matches the clue. Write the word.

1. not big — lleitt — **little**
2. from one side to the other — scasor — **across**
3. use it with thread — deenel — **needle**
4. in front — aadhe — **ahead**
5. a color — lerpup — **purple**

Notes for Home: Your child wrote words with the schwa sound spelled *a* or consonant + *le*. **Home Activity:** Have your child tell a story using the words *poodle, table, noodle, about,* and *alone*.

114

Review Plural *-s* and *-es*

Add *-s* or *-es* to a word to show more than one.
nurse—nurse**s**   inch—inch**es**
fox—fox**es**   bush—bush**es**   bus—bus**es**

Circle *s* or *es* to show how to make each picture name mean more than one.

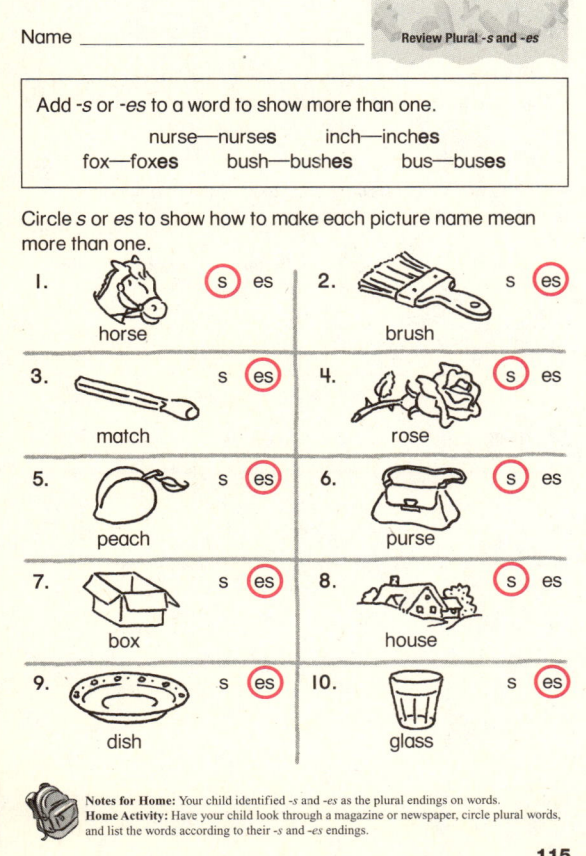

1. horse — (s) es
2. brush — s (es)
3. match — s (es)
4. rose — (s) es
5. peach — s (es)
6. purse — (s) es
7. box — s (es)
8. house — (s) es
9. dish — s (es)
10. glass — s (es)

Notes for Home: Your child identified *-s* and *-es* as the plural endings on words. **Home Activity:** Have your child look through a magazine or newspaper, circle plural words, and list the words according to their *-s* and *-es* endings.

115

Long *a*: *ei*, *eigh*

The long *a* sound can be spelled *ei* as in *reindeer* or *eigh* as in *eight*.

Circle the word that has the same vowel sound as the picture name. Underline the letters that spell the vowel sound in the word.

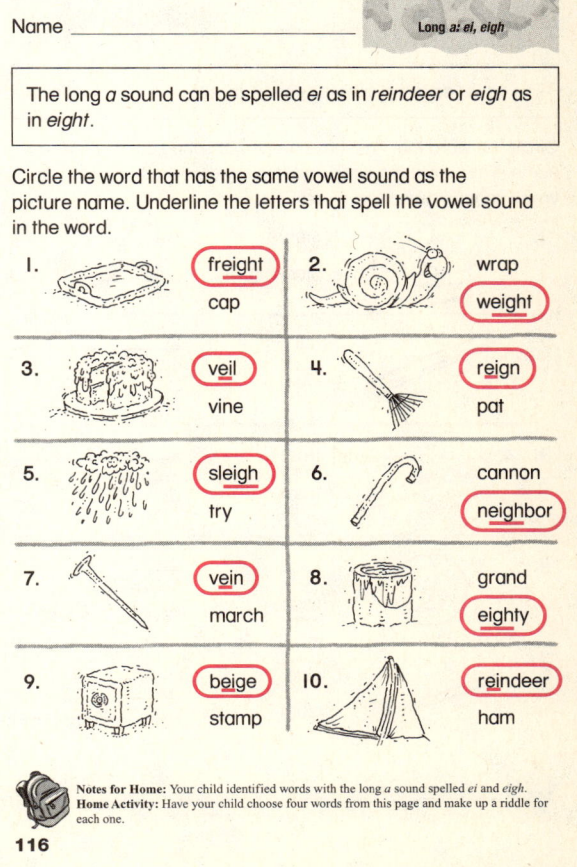

1. (freight) / cap
2. wrap / (weight)
3. (veil) / vine
4. (reign) / pat
5. (sleigh) / try
6. cannon / (neighbor)
7. (vein) / march
8. grand / (eighty)
9. (beige) / stamp
10. (reindeer) / ham

Notes for Home: Your child identified words with the long *a* sound spelled *ei* and *eigh*. **Home Activity:** Have your child choose four words from this page and make up a riddle for each one.

116

Answers 179

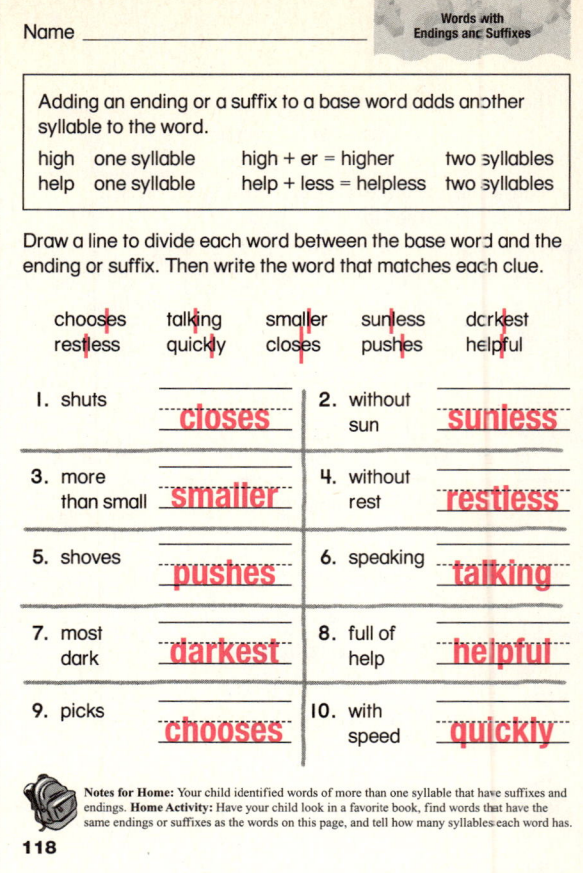

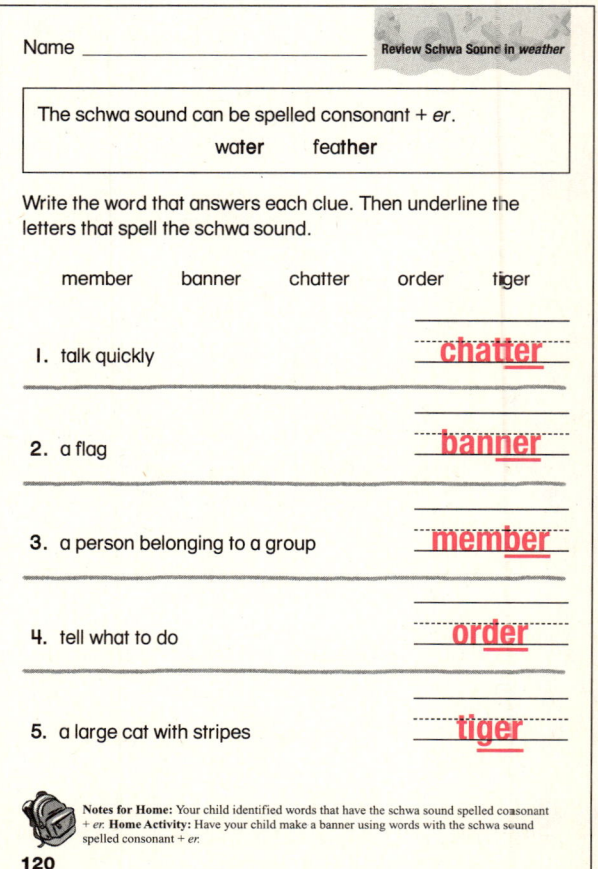

Page 121

Pattern ex

The letters *ex* spell the beginning sounds in these words.
explore   **ex**cite

Write a word from the box in place of the underlined word or words.

| exit | next | explain | Texas | exact |

1. Austin is the capital of a large state. — **Texas**
2. The sign showed him the way out. — **exit**
3. My watch tells correct time. — **exact**
4. Her birthday is the following week. — **next**
5. Can you tell how the machine works? — **explain**

Notes for Home: Your child wrote words with the *ex* pattern. Home Activity: Together with your child look through a magazine or newspaper for other words with the *ex* pattern. Make a list of the words you find.

Page 122

Pattern ex

In words like *exercise* and *expert*, the letters *ex* stand for the beginning sounds.

Add *ex* to the letters to finish the word. Write the word.

1. the ind **ex** of the book — **index**
2. the state of T **ex** as — **Texas**
3. n **ex** t in line — **next**
4. **ex** it from the room — **exit**
5. an **ex** act copy — **exact**
6. an **ex** tra pair of socks — **extra**
7. a good **ex** ample — **example**
8. an **ex** pert in math — **expert**
9. everyone **ex** cept me — **except**
10. **ex** plore the cave — **explore**

Notes for Home: Your child completed words with the *ex* pattern. Home Activity: Challenge your child to tell a story using the words *explain, excellent, extra, example,* and *experiment*.

Page 123

Prefixes un-, dis-, re-

A prefix is a word part added to the beginning of a word. Adding a prefix like *un-*, *dis-*, or *re-* changes the meaning of the word.

un + happy = **un**happy   not happy, the opposite of *happy*
dis + loyal = **dis**loyal   not loyal, the opposite of *loyal*
re + wind = **re**wind   to wind again

Add the prefix to the underlined word. Write the new word.

1. (dis) to not like — **dislike**
2. (dis) the opposite of obey — **disobey**
3. (re) to fill again — **refill**
4. (un) the opposite of safe — **unsafe**
5. (un) not lucky — **unlucky**

Notes for Home: Your child wrote words with the prefixes *un-*, *dis-*, and *re-*. Home Activity: Have your child choose a word from the page and draw a picture to show how the meaning changed when the prefix *un-*, *dis-*, or *re-* was added.

Page 124

Review Long a: ei, eigh

The letters *ei* and *eigh* spell the long *a* sound in *rein* and *sleigh*.

Unscramble the letters to make a word from the list that has the long *a* sound spelled *ei* or *eigh*. Write the word.

| eight | freight | veil | beige | weight |

1. The bride wore a lace *leiv*. — **veil**
2. He washed his *geeib* shirt. — **beige**
3. The bowl held *tigeh* eggs. — **eight**
4. The *rifthge* train hauled coal. — **freight**
5. What is the *gwieth* of that box? — **weight**

Notes for Home: Your child identified words with the long *a* sound spelled *ei* and *eigh*. Home Activity: Have your child rewrite each sentence on this page as a question and underline the long *a* words.

Answers **181**

Worksheet 125 — Words with Endings and Suffixes

Adding an ending or a suffix to a base word usually adds another syllable to the word.

match	one syllable
match + es = matches	two syllables
cold	one syllable
cold + er = colder	two syllables

Follow the signs to make a new word. Write the word. Then in the box write the number of syllables you hear.

1. finish + es — **finishes** — 3
2. run + ing — **running** — 2
3. swift + ly — **swiftly** — 2
4. beauty + ful — **beautiful** — 3
5. hopped − ed + ing — **hopping** — 2

Notes for Home: Your child identified words of more than one syllable that have suffixes and endings. **Home Activity:** Have your child add an ending or suffix to *forget*, *wish*, and *sudden* and tell how many syllables each new word has.

125

Worksheet 126 — Long e: ie, ey

The long *e* vowel sound in *niece* is spelled *ie*.
The long *e* vowel sound in *valley* is spelled *ey*.

Draw a line to match each picture with its name. Circle the letters that stand for the long *e* sound in each word.

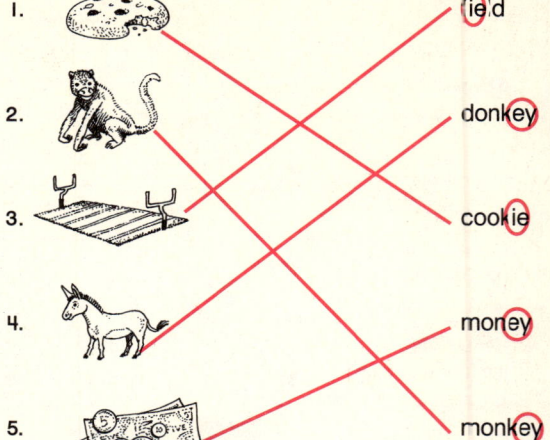

1. — cookie
2. — monkey
3. — field
4. — donkey
5. — money

Notes for Home: Your child identified words that have the long *e* vowel sound spelled *ie* and *ey*. **Home Activity:** Have your child choose two words from this page and make up a riddle for each one.

126

Worksheet 127 — Long e: ie, ey

In the word *grief*, the letters *ie* spell the long *e* vowel sound.
In the word *trolley*, the letters *ey* spell the long *e* vowel sound.

Underline the words that have the long *e* sound spelled *ie* or *ey*. Then follow the directions.

alley	shy	chief	field	team
brief	pulley	niece	they	piece
money	obey	beige	key	hockey

1. Write the word that rhymes with *shield*. — **field**
2. Write the word that names a relative. — **niece**
3. Write the word that names something that opens a lock. — **key**
4. Write the word that names a game played on ice. — **hockey**
5. Write the word that means a part of something. — **piece**

Notes for Home: Your child identified words that have the long *e* vowel sound spelled *ie* and *ey*. **Home Activity:** Challenge your child to think of clues for the five underlined words that were not written on the page.

127

Worksheet 128 — Consonants gh, ph, lf /f/

The *f* sound can be spelled *gh*, *ph*, and *lf*.

cough   gopher   halfway

Write the word that answers the question. Circle the letters that stand for the *f* sound.

1. Does sandpaper feel rough or enough? — **rough**
2. Have you had enough or tough when you are full? — **enough**
3. Does a dolphin or an elephant live in the ocean? — **dolphin**
4. Do you use a phone or a graph to call a friend? — **phone**
5. Is a calf or a nephew a baby cow? — **calf**

Notes for Home: Your child identified words that have the *f* sound spelled *gh*, *ph*, and *lf*. **Home Activity:** Have your child write sentences using the words *tough*, *alphabet*, and *golf*.

128

---

182 Answers

Review Pattern *ex*

The letters *ex* can be at the beginning, in the middle, or at the end of words.

Find and circle the *ex* words in the puzzle. Then write the *ex* word that goes with each meaning clue.

examine
extra
index
explode
next

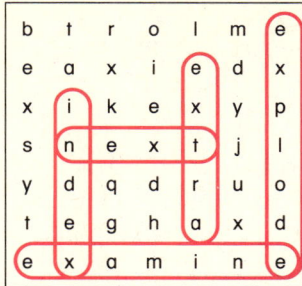

1. following — **next**
2. part of a book — **index**
3. look at carefully — **examine**
4. to burst — **explode**
5. more than enough — **extra**

Notes for Home: Your child wrote words with the *ex* pattern. Home Activity: Have your child write a question using each of the *ex* words on this page.

129

Prefixes *-un, -dis, -re*

The prefixes *un-* and *dis-* mean *not* or *opposite of*.
The prefix *re-* means *to do again*.

the opposite of *like* — **un**like
not respectful — **dis**respectful
to play again — **re**play

Add the prefix to the base word to form a new word. Use the new words to complete the sentences.

(un) wrap (dis) honest (re) load
(un) ripe (re) heat

1. The **dishonest** person stole the money.
2. Can you **reheat** the soup?
3. Is that green banana **unripe**?
4. Jeff wants to **unwrap** his present.
5. The driver will **reload** the truck.

Notes for Home: Your child wrote words with the prefixes *un-, dis-,* and *re-*. Home Activity: Have your child add *un-, dis-,* or *re-* to these words: *kind, agree, build*.

130

Long *e: ei*

In the word *receipt*, the letters *ei* spell the long *e* vowel sound.

Add *ei* to the letters to finish the word. Write the word.

1. Flying kites is Mike's l**e i**sure activity. — **leisure**
2. You get prot**e i**n from meat. — **protein**
3. She painted the c**e i**ling. — **ceiling**
4. Did you rec**e i**ve a gift? — **receive**
5. The player s**e i**zed the ball. — **seized**

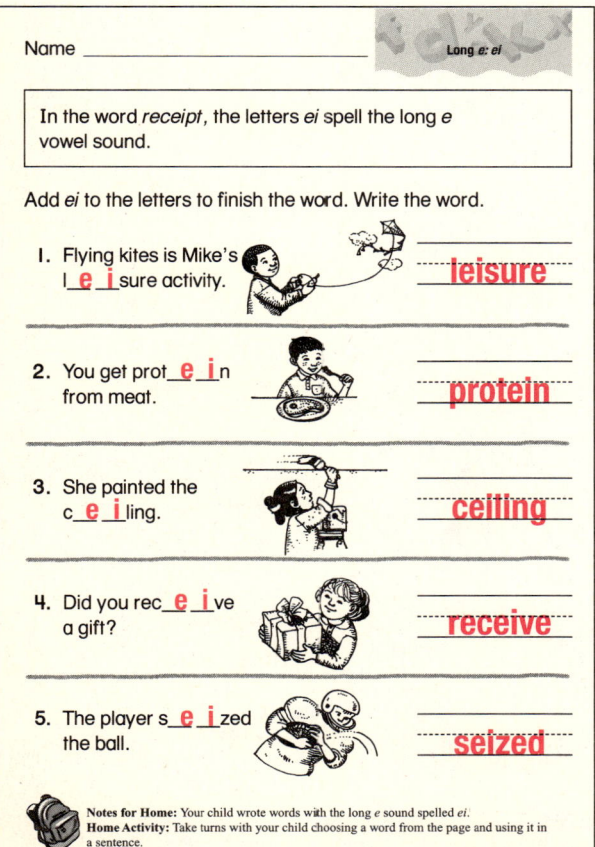

Notes for Home: Your child wrote words with the long *e* sound spelled *ei*. Home Activity: Take turns with your child choosing a word from the page and using it in a sentence.

131

Long *e: ei*

The long *e* vowel sound can be spelled *ei* as in *protein*.

Follow the directions. Use the words from the box. Then circle the letters that stand for the long *e* sound.

| ceiling | seize | receipt | leisure | receive |

1. Write the word that names time you spend not working. — **leisure**
2. Write the word that means "get." — **receive**
3. Write the word that names part of a room. — **ceiling**
4. Write the word that means "grab." — **seize**
5. Write the word that names the paper you get when you buy something. — **receipt**

Notes for Home: Your child identified words with the long *e* sound spelled *ei*. Home Activity: Scramble the letters of each word in the box and have your child unscramble and write the words.

132

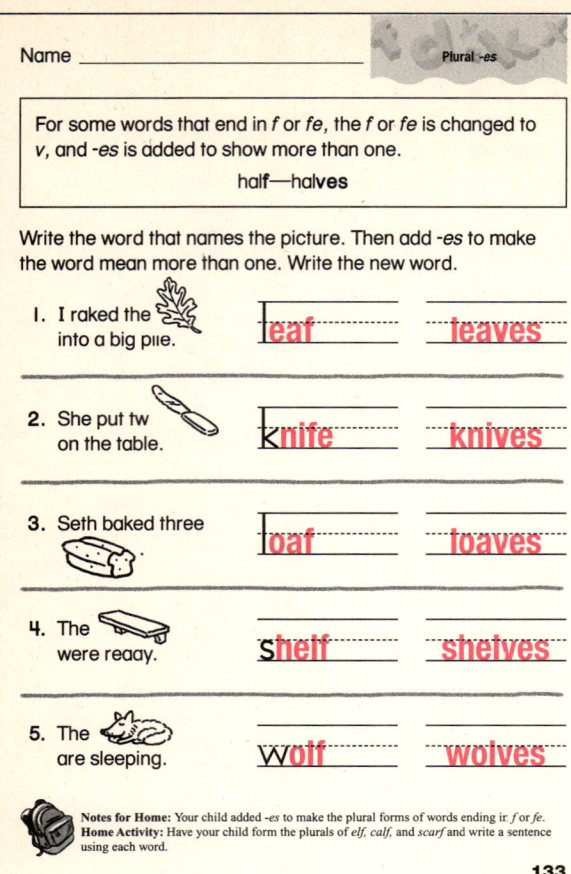
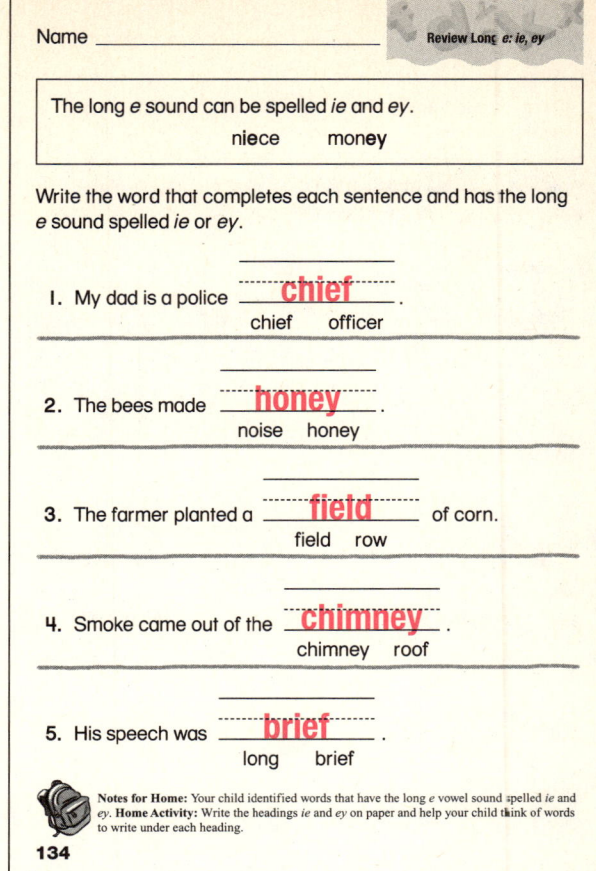
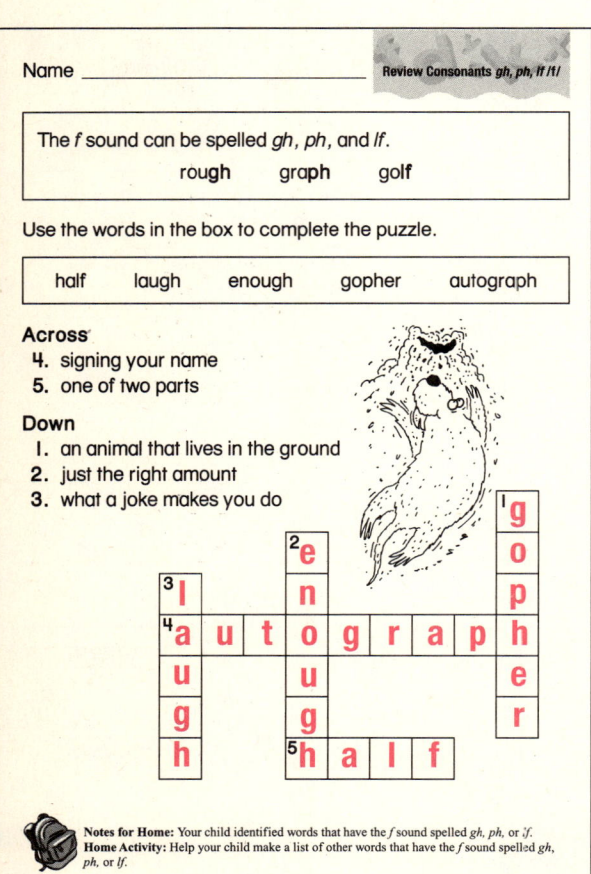
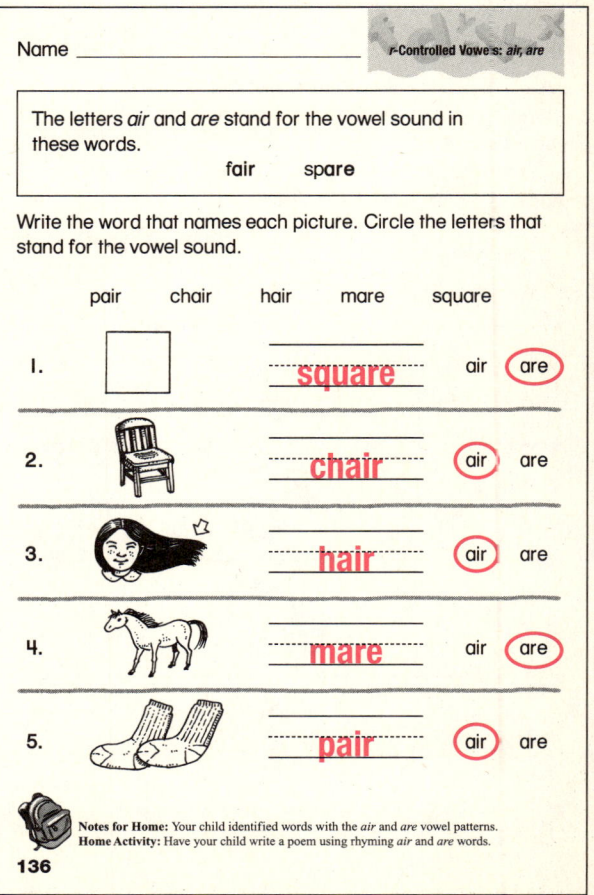

Page 137 — r-Controlled Vowels: air, are

In words like *hair* and *dare*, the letters *air* and *are* stand for the vowel sound.

Write the word that matches the meaning and has the vowel sound in *hair*. Circle the letters that spell the vowel sound.

1. to look at something — gaze / stare — **st(are)**
2. something to sit on — chair / couch — **ch(air)**
3. to fix something — repair / mend — **rep(air)**
4. to make a loud sound — shout / blare — **bl(are)**
5. two that go together — pair / couple — **p(air)**

Notes for Home: Your child identified words with the *air* and *are* vowel patterns. **Home Activity:** Have your child make a list of words that rhyme with *care*.

Page 138 — Consonants: dge /j/

The letters *dge* spell the *j* sound in *hedge*.

Write the word from the box that completes each sentence. Underline the letters that spell the ending *j* sound.

bridge   judge   fudge   ledge   badge

1. The police officer wore a shiny **badge**.
2. A new **bridge** was built over the river.
3. Sara put nuts in the **fudge**.
4. I set the plant on the window **ledge**.
5. The **judge** spoke to the jury.

Notes for Home: Your child wrote words in which /j/ is spelled *dge*. **Home Activity:** Have your child write a tongue twister using the words *badge*, *budge*, and *bridge*.

Page 139 — Review Long e: ei

The letters *ei* spell the long *e* sound in *receipt*.

Find five words in the puzzle with the long *e* sound spelled *ei*. Circle each word in the puzzle. Then write the word.

1. **receive**
2. **receipt**
3. **leisure**
4. **ceiling**
5. **deceive**

Order may vary.

Notes for Home: Your child identified words that have the long *e* vowel sound spelled *ei*. **Home Activity:** Give a clue for each of the circled words and have your child name the *ei* word that goes with the clue.

Page 140 — Review Plural -es

To form the plural of some words ending in *f* or *fe*, *f* or *fe* is changed to *v*, and *-es* is added.

wife — wives

Write the plural form of the underlined word.

1. The loaf of bread was freshly baked. — **loaves**
2. The wolf howled at the moon. — **wolves**
3. The dictionary is on that shelf. — **shelves**

Write the singular form of the underlined word.

4. Did the tree's leaves turn red? — **leaf**
5. Carl put the knives next to the spoons. — **knife**

Notes for Home: Your child wrote the plural and singular forms of words ending in *f* and *fe*. **Home Activity:** Encourage your child to write a short story using as many plural words as possible from this page.

Answers **185**

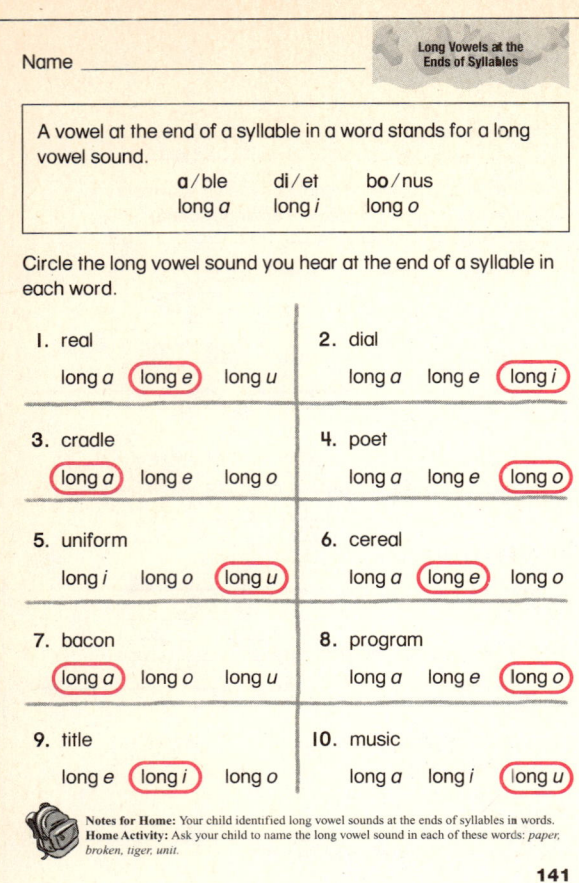

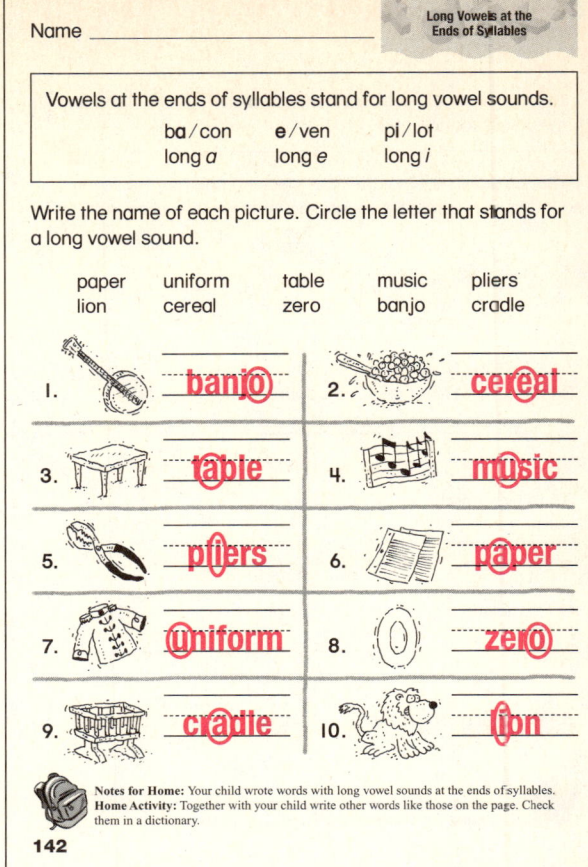

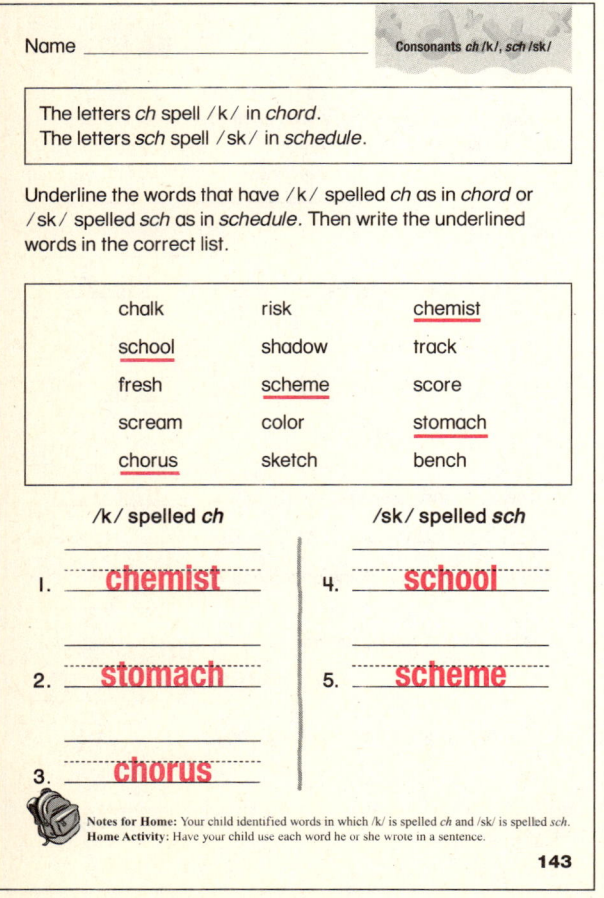

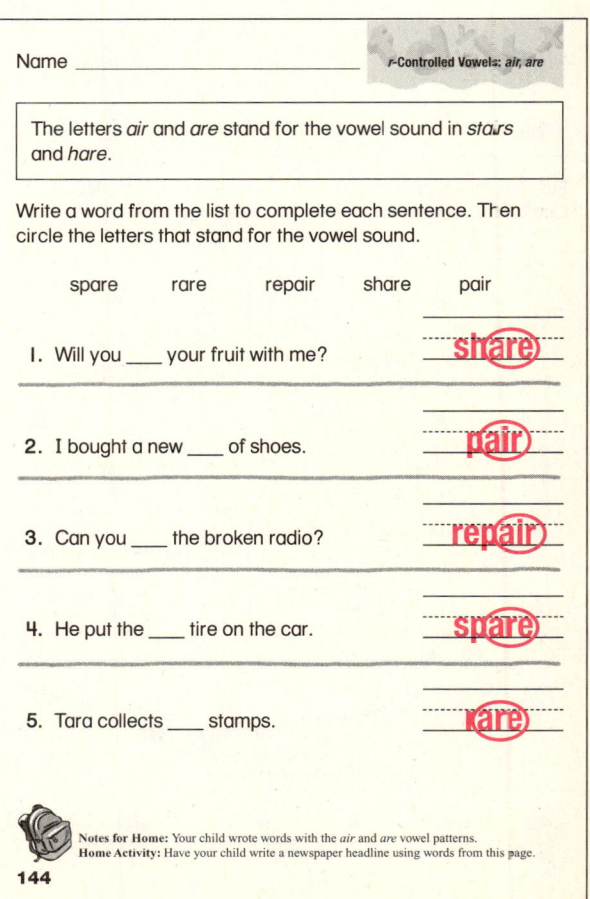

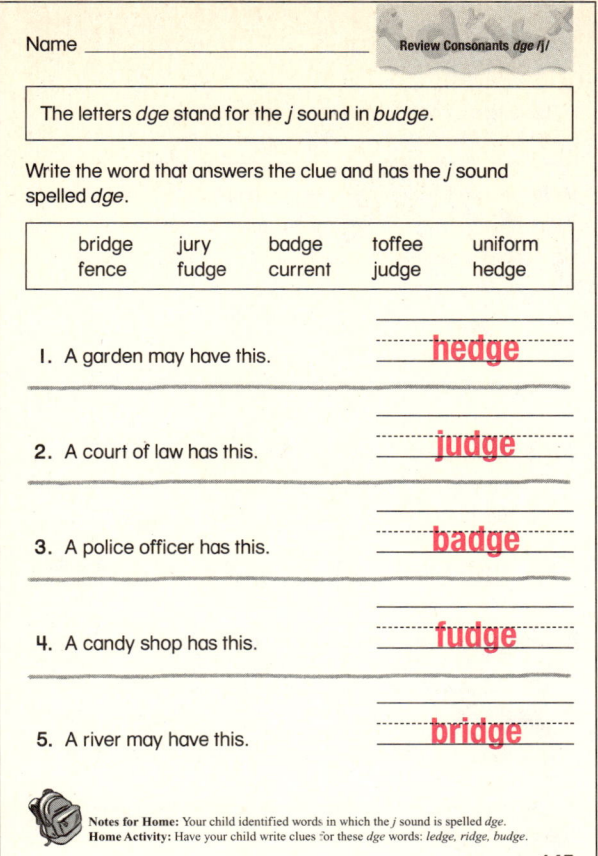

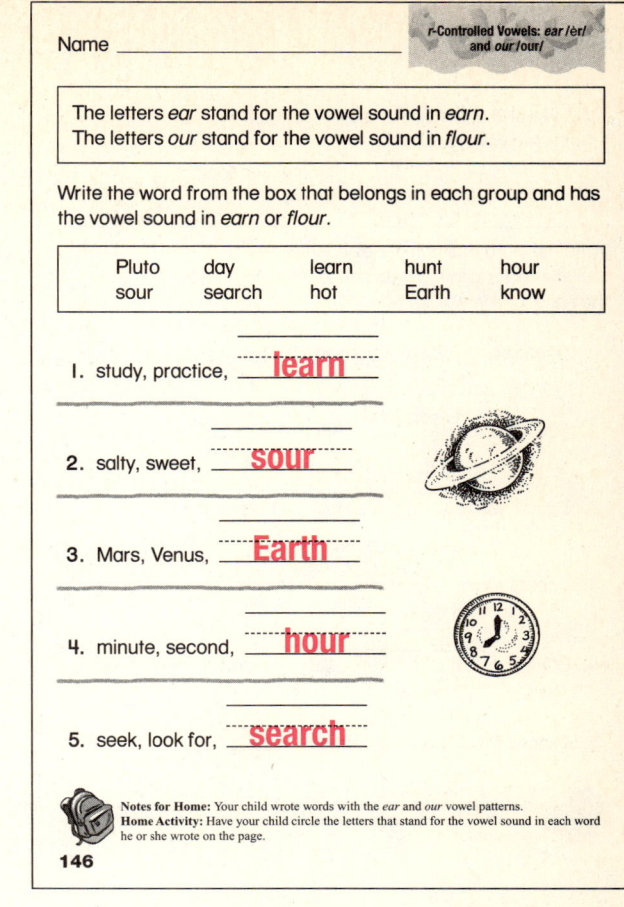

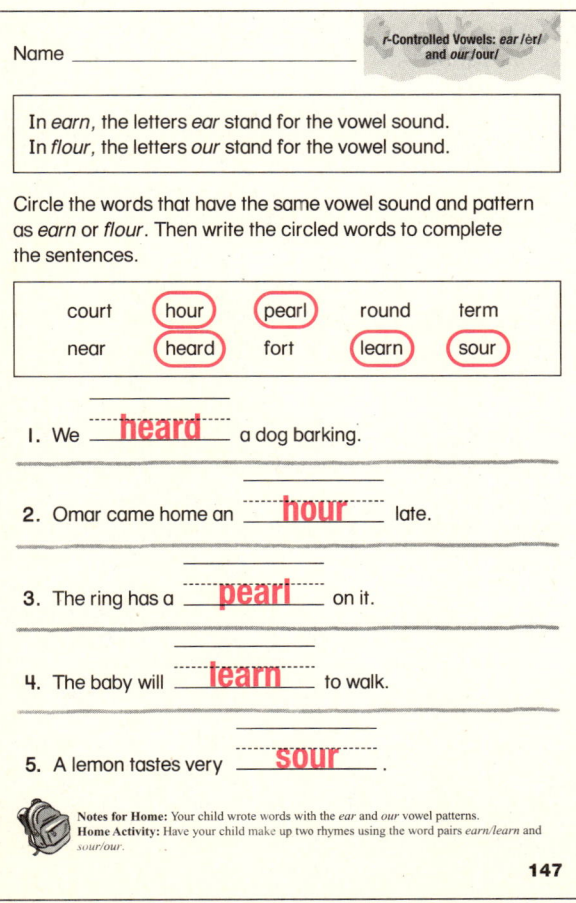

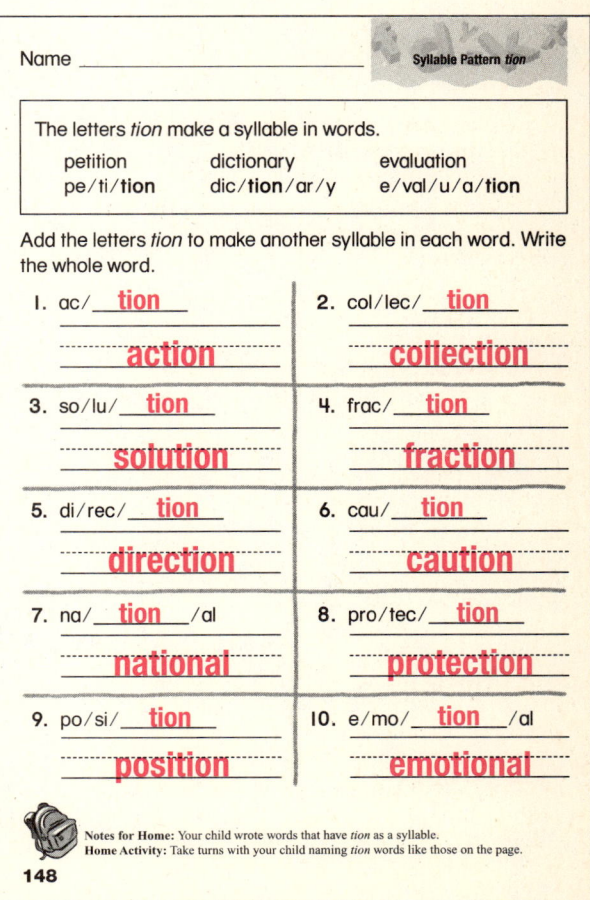

Name _____   Review Long Vowels at the Ends of Syllables

If a vowel is at the end of a syllable in a word, it can stand for a long vowel sound.

  ve/to long *e* long *o*
  tor/na/do long *a* long *o*

Write the word that completes each sentence. Circle each letter that stands for a long vowel sound. *Hint:* Each word has more than one long vowel sound.

 stereo idea radio piano video

1. A local __r(a)d(i)(o)__ station is having a talent contest.

2. I could win a __st(e)r(e)(o)__ with speakers.

3. I could win a __v(i)d(e)(o)__ camera.

4. But I have no __(i)d(e)(a)__ what I can do.

5. I know! I'll play a song on the __p(i)(a)n(o)__.

Notes for Home: Your child wrote words with long vowel sounds at the ends of syllables.
Home Activity: Have your child write a sentence using at least two of the long vowel words on the page.

149

Name _____   Review Consonants *ch* /k/, *sch* /sk/

The letters *ch* can spell /k/ as in *chemist*.
The letters *sch* can spell /sk/ as in *scheme*.

Write the words to complete the paragraph. Circle the letters that spell /k/ as in *chemist* or /sk/ as in *scheme*.

 chord schedule school stomach chorus

I have a busy (1.) __s(ch)edule__ on Tuesdays.

From 8 until 3:30, I am at (2.) __s(ch)ool__. Then I sing

in a (3.) __(ch)orus__. This Tuesday I was so busy I

missed lunch. At practice, when Mrs. Nuñez played a

(4.) __(ch)ord__ on the piano, my (5.) __stoma(ch)__

growled really loud—right on cue! Everyone laughed.

Notes for Home: Your child wrote words in which *ch* spelled /k/ or *sch* spelled /sk/.
Home Activity: Together with your child make up a funny story using the *ch* and *sch* words on the page.

150